WHAT PEOPLE ARE SAYING ABOUT WALT HILL AND *AMAZED AGAIN*

"Walt's teaching, preaching, and writing have profoundly impacted my life for more than two decades. He is not only a voice for this generation, but also a trusted friend. In moments when I felt like giving up or changing direction, Walt has been there. Faithful, and Spirit led. He always has a word to help me realign my steps. His encouragement and wisdom have played a significant role in leading me to plant our church and where I am today in my leadership journey. I am forever grateful for his love, friendship, and unwavering voice."

Bryan Lamoureux, Lead Pastor, Reverb Church, St. Augustine, Florida

"I have personally known Walt for over 25 years. I have had him come to our church several times to minister the Word. He always brings incredible revelation, encouragement, and the profundity that he has been known for all the years that we have been friends. His experiences and deep understanding of the Scriptures challenge people to higher standards and following Jesus more intimately."

Dan Colvin, Senior Pastor, Center City Church, Greensboro, North Carolina

"I've had the privilege of knowing Pastor Walt since 2013, and his life and ministry have been a consistent testament to his deep relationship with Christ and his boldness in challenging the religious status quo. In Montana he served as a proven prophetic voice, able to see and hear what God is doing, and fostering unity between Native American believers and non-natives in a city often marked by division. As a Biblical teacher, reformer, and conduit of revival, Pastor Walt's ministry encourages believers to pursue authentic faith and a deeper relationship with Christ."

Jeremy Stands Over Bull, Associate Leader, Arrow Creek International Ministries

"We have known Walter Hill for just over 20 years. In that time I have known him to always be Spirit led, with the courage to say it like it is. He loves the Word of God and has a great desire for believers to truly understand it. He is kind, and he loves his family. Even though he often lives a few states away, I consider him a good friend and my brother in the Lord."

Reverend Dan Fryer, DCF Ministries

"Walt is real. He is kind to everyone, no matter where they are in life. He cares about people, and he always puts forth the effort to hear them, and really listen. He does not pretend to be something for appearances, and he shoots straight. He works consistently to be a light in our community."

Richard and Kasey Walker, Here to Help Wyoming Foundation, Neighbors Feeding Neighbors

AMAZED AGAIN

RECLAIMING CHRIST'S JOY IN A FADING WORLD

WALTER HILL

Amazed Again
Reclaiming Christ's Joy in a Fading World
Walter Hill © 2025

The publisher supports copyright and the sharing of thoughts and ideas it enables. Thank you for buying an authorized edition of this book and honoring our request to obtain permission for any use of any part of this publication, whether reproduced, transmitted in any form or by any means, electronic, mechanical, photocopying, recording, or otherwise, or stored in a retrieval system. Your honorable actions support all writers and allow the publishing industry to continue publishing books for all readers. All rights reserved.

While the publisher and author have used their best efforts in preparing this book, they make no representations or warranties with respect to the accuracy or completeness of this book and specifically disclaim any implied warranties of merchantability or fitness for a particular purpose. No warranty may be created or extended by sales representatives or written sales materials. The stories and interviews in this book are true although the names and identifiable information may have been changed to maintain confidentiality.

The publisher and author shall have neither liability nor responsibility to any person or entity with respect to loss of profit or property, damage, or injury caused or alleged to be caused directly or indirectly by the information contained in this book.

Scripture quotations marked (NLT) are taken from the Holy Bible, New Living Translation, copyright © 1996, 2004, 2015 by Tyndale House Foundation. Used by permission of Tyndale House Publishers, Inc., Carol Stream, Illinois 60188. All rights reserved.

Scripture quotations marked (NKJV) are taken from the New King James Version®. Copyright © 1982 by Thomas Nelson. Used by permission. All rights reserved.

Softcover ISBN: 978-1-61206-336-2
eBook ISBN: 978-1-61206-337-9

To purchase this book at quantity discounts, contact Aloha Publishing at alohapublishing@gmail.com

Published by

Printed in the United States of America

DEDICATION

To the "Happy Singing Guy"—the one whose unwavering joy and contagious faith lit the way for so many of us to rediscover the beauty of knowing Jesus. Your songs of praise and your unshakable joy have left an enduring mark on hearts, reminding us all that joy in the Lord is a treasure worth pursuing.

And to you, dear reader—this book is for you. May it inspire you to reclaim the joy of your salvation, to sing with gratitude, and to walk in the hope and fullness that comes from knowing Christ. May your journey through these pages lead you to a deeper, lasting joy that overflows into every corner of your life.

CONTENTS

A Note From the Author	11
Foreword	13
Introduction: The Fade	17
Chapter One: The Beginning	31
Chapter Two: The Source	41
Chapter Three: The Word	51
Chapter Four: The Kingdom	71
Chapter Five: The Family	85
Chapter Six: Family Matters	95
Chapter Seven: The Adversary	111
Chapter Eight: The Sacrifice	125
Chapter Nine: The Spirit	135
Chapter Ten: The Songs	149
Chapter Eleven: The Towel	159
Chapter Twelve: The Meal	175
Chapter Thirteen: The Secret Place	185
Chapter Fourteen: Become Amazed Again	199
Conclusion	213
About the Author	219
Connect With Walt	221

A NOTE FROM THE AUTHOR

Dear Reader,

If you picked up this book, you are most likely interested in finding your lost joy. That is wonderful because Jesus wants to fill your life with His joy! Even if, in this moment of your life, that seems a lofty or even unattainable goal, let me assure you, He is able to do it. Most often, the only work we need to do is align our lives to the truth found in His Word. He is our Teacher and shows us how to do that if we listen.

This book has been put together to help you. Consider it a road map of sorts. The chapters can lead you step-by-step, and with each step, more joy will come into view. Some of it will challenge you, just like it did me, but the journey is worth it. How do I know that?

In the world of faith-based publication today, there are two main sources of material. Individuals working toward their doctoral degree often convert their thesis project into a book. It is solid information but based on their theories going through school. Most often, the rest of the published material is a written version of a teaching series delivered at a larger ministry. That is also solid material but delivered to their audience, and then shared with the rest of us. This book is different. This is the result of a 25-year journey—through the school of life—and the lessons learned along the way. Learning to find my way back to joy after deaths in my family, long-term illnesses in loved ones, divisive people wounding people we cared about, and personal attacks based on falsehoods is the foundation of what you are holding in your hands. This is not a theory. This proven pathway has worked for me and can work for you as well.

My prayer is that you and Jesus connect profoundly, and His joy floods your soul!

—Walt

FOREWORD

This book is an invitation to experience joy, regardless of your circumstances and throughout every season of life. Walt's vulnerability guides us through his journey of discovering the joy of Christ, losing that joy, and ultimately rediscovering it. The road he traveled can become a pathway for anyone who finds themselves in a joyless place. Along the way, he gently and skillfully directs us to God's word, where we can rediscover our true foundation. It is a path of real, relatable, simple truth that makes your heart sigh with relief as refreshing joy begins to emerge within your soul. Truly seeing Jesus and connecting with Him at the heart level is where genuine joy flows.

Just as a good physician prescribes the right remedy for an illness, this experienced pastor applies verse after verse to our lives. I felt my eyes gently drawn to Jesus, smiling as I read and newly inspired by the sweet presence of the Holy Spirit. His storytelling ability takes us on a shared journey.

Walt is a friend and fellow pastor. We've shared meals, ministry, heartaches, and our passions. He is not only a lover of Jesus but also cares deeply for His people. He is as authentic as they come and one of the most talented yet humble people you'll ever meet. In this book, Walt candidly shares his own life lessons with us. *Amazed Again* will be a blessing to those who take the time to read it. Thanks, Walt!

Jamie Gillentine
Lead Pastor, Dillon Vineyard Church, Montana

———

"We are not made for the mountaintops;
we are made for the valley. The moment we begin to
experience fading joy, it often reveals that we are looking
to the experience rather than to God Himself."

—Oswald Chambers

INTRODUCTION

THE FADE

Joy fades. That is one of the more brutal truths of our human journey. We learn this about ourselves from the earliest days of our life. As an infant, we were thrilled and giggling at the game of peek-a-boo, but in short order, it is no longer fascinating, and we are no longer laughing. A toy we unwrapped at Christmas to our own squeals of delight is discarded into the corner of our room before summer break. We carry this ever-degrading level of joy and satisfaction into our adult lives. The car we leased, the home we purchased, the job we fought for, and even the person we married can lose their appeal and attraction until they no longer bring us joy. What is wrong with us?

Recently I entered a home to initiate some marriage counseling for a middle-aged couple. As I waited in the living room area for the wife to make her entrance, I glanced at the photos that adorned the walls and the top of an old upright piano. As is fairly normal, everyone in the pictures looked very happy. I took special note of a particularly sweet one where the photographer had captured the exact moment the husband presented his wife with a special gift. Her face was frozen full of laughter and an enormous smile. When she walked into the room, she was presenting a very different expression. What followed was bitter and spiteful as they both presented their list of observed shortcomings in one another and concluded the marriage must be over because neither was "happy anymore." I found myself thinking: *How does this happen to us?*

In our own lives, it was amazing to watch one of our children journey through college, in multiple settings, working diligently toward a career. The first week of their job, that career was declared "perfect" but only two years later was announced as "terrible." My wife once surprised me with an amazing sports car that was far nicer than anything we had ever owned. We are not wealthy—usually leaning more towards broke, actually—but she had found an amazing deal, and we were able to get it. For the first few months I treated it like a precious flower that was easily damaged. I washed it all the time and maintained the interior like someone important was waiting to get in for a ride. But, you guessed it. By the second year of ownership, it was just a car. The bugs on the front were allowed to stay longer than twenty minutes and the interior had a fast-food bag, or three, on the floorboard. It was the same car and I was the same driver but the joy of owning it was gone. What happens to us?

It will be difficult to acknowledge for most of us, but even our joy as parents seems to fade away with time and attitude problems. Most of us would agree that our hearts were filled with a joy that we didn't even know was possible when we first held our children. They were perfect in our sight and tears streamed down most of our faces. We can't imagine loving anyone or anything more and our hearts were filled with pride and gratitude. Forward the timeline to our sixteen-year-old yelling at us because we have questioned the tenth missed curfew, or we are standing beside them in court when they simply cannot stop making bad decisions, and most of that initial joy is gone. We tell ourselves we still love them, but it has become a decision rather than a feeling. How does this happen to us?

Joy is a powerful force in the human heart. Numerous Bible lessons speak of this and challenge us all to walk in our joy. If it was as easy as knowing joy is described in the pages of the Scripture, there would be nothing more to discuss. I could simply remind you of a verse or two at this point and you would go on your way rejoicing.

Our problem is the very apparent disconnect between what we know and believe and how we feel and behave.

This diversity of experience was spoken of by the Apostle Paul in one of his most personal and vulnerable expositions.

> "I have discovered this principle of life—that when I want to do what is right, I inevitably do what is wrong. I love God's law with all my heart. But there is another power within me that is at war with my mind. This power makes me a slave to the sin that is still within me. Oh, what a miserable person I am! Who will free me from this life that is dominated by sin and death?"
>
> Romans 7:21-24 NLT

Does this sound like anyone you know? For me, it feels like a journal entry for the guy looking at me in the mirror in the morning. Two versions of me seem to be in conflict all the time. Without doing an immediate deep dive into all the theology of this situation, I will pause instead to let us think on this for a moment. Is the fact that joy fades and dwindles and vanishes away, even though we are looking at good and beautiful blessings, a part of the "other power" that is at work within? This is like an ongoing decay and corruption that seems to stay with us no matter how many times we attend church. When we consider how many regretful life decisions would not have happened if we were simply content and joyful, the potential importance of this comes into focus.

Imagine with me how wonderful life would be if we could hold on to our joy. What if happiness endured? How much peace would we walk in daily if we held on to contentment and joy in our situation rather than falling into the trap of comparison and resentment? The end result would be happier homes and more healthy relationships. It would result in more consistent decision-making and more goals actually achieved. All of this would significantly increase our witness to this fallen world as they begin to see more of the hope that we carry within us! (1 Peter 3:15)

There is someone who can help us. The majority of us already know Him. He is as close as our own heart and has unlimited love for us. Jesus is the answer to this dilemma. Paul resolved himself that this was the source of his victory over his own "dark side."

THE FADE

Imagine with me how wonderful life would be if we could hold on to our joy.

"But there is another power within me that is at war with my mind. This power makes me a slave to the sin that is still within me. Oh, what a miserable person I am! Who will free me from this life that is dominated by sin and death? Thank God! The answer is in Jesus Christ our Lord."

Romans 7:23-25 NLT

Jesus is the answer to overcoming this *other power* that is working within all of us to corrupt and pollute our joy. He is the answer to overcoming all the corruption that is flowing out of our old nature. We will explore this further but in a simple and direct bullet point, our victory is found in more of Jesus rather than more stubborn effort and striving in our own strength. Our future does not have to be forcing a smile onto our face out of a sense of religious duty. We can walk in a genuine joy that is flowing from the abiding presence of Jesus within us. We can access a joy and strength that endures time and challenges and shines like a light in the darkness of this broken world. Jesus made us all this promise as He was raising up the original disciples.

"I have told you these things so that you will be filled with my joy. Yes, your joy will overflow!"

John 15:11 NLT

Because of the influence of religious thinking in our nation and the nations of the world, most individuals do not immediately associate Jesus with *joy*. Depending on background and experience, the name of Jesus may invoke all sorts of other feelings and thought processes. Most people immediately merge the concepts of *church* and *Christ* together and then respond to both like they are one. If *church people* were unloving or hypocritical, then we choose to stay away from Jesus altogether even though He didn't do anything wrong. If most *church people* we know appear sour and grumpy about the state of the world, we assume walking with Jesus must contribute to how they are acting. This is a mistake. *Church* is always an imperfect effort of mankind to organize and serve Jesus as a group. Made up of imperfect people, the resulting efforts and expressions are also never perfect. Christ Himself is perfect in every single way. When He promises us access to His joy, we should be lining up to find how to receive all we can.

The influence of religion has had one other effect that has influenced the rest of our spiritual culture in a detrimental way. In the same way, our joy is often fading and diminished in every other area of our lives, we find that our joy in knowing Christ diminishes as well. For those who have truly been *born again* and come into relationship with Jesus, there should be joy! Scripture speaks of this so often it will take this entire project to look at all the references. JOY is supposed to be at the core of who Christians are. Paul made this abundantly clear in several letters as he instructed the first Christians.

"*Always be joyful.*"

1 Thessalonians 5:16 NLT

THE FADE

"Always be full of joy in the Lord. I say it again—rejoice!"

Philippians 4:4 NLT

"For the Kingdom of God is not a matter of what we eat or drink, but of living a life of goodness and peace and joy in the Holy Spirit."

Romans 14:17 NLT

Sadly, a very recognizable pattern in modern circles is the same fading and diminishing of joy in this area that we see infecting us in other areas. Most people will tell you they were the most excited and joyful about Jesus when they first came to faith. The longer they attend church, the more they find that joy and happiness are being replaced by a sense of duty and performance. The more experienced we become in matters of Biblical insight and learning, the more serious and somber we appear to become. This pattern makes no sense at all. Our knowledge and growth as the disciples of Jesus should be producing *more* joy! Our understanding of the Kingdom of God should be leading us toward more aspects of truth and grace in Christ, and our lives should be reflecting more of that goodness, peace, and joy. We should be expanding in joy. Is this your experience?

When I first came to faith in Christ, His joy filled my heart.

Joy felt so foreign to me at that time that I often just sat in the quiet and took stock of what I was lacking. Joy had replaced hopelessness and worthlessness, and I could tangibly feel the absence of that darkness. My future seemed open and possible rather than living each day already sure "I would never amount to anything." The relationship I was discovering each day in Christ was swallowing all of the rejection I had so often felt from people. Instead of a gaping hole in my heart, I felt a sense of belonging and life that was truly remarkable. Then I got serious about attending church. Like so many of you, I was informed that church is where we go to have connection to God. Slowly the wonderful joy I had carried in my soul began to be replaced with *religious* stuff.

One of the most remarkable people in the little church I started becoming a part of was the song leader. He was always happy about Jesus. He sang every song with a huge smile on his face and he was always happy to sing the song several more times if everyone would let him. In contrast to him, the pastor and his wife seemed very tired, bitter, and serious. I now understand those dynamics better, but the simple truth of this observation is that the joy in the song leader was attractive, and the lack of it in the others was very apparent as well. Why was he happy about God all the time? Why did the people teaching us the Bible and giving us all the answers lack that same joy? My young mind reasoned they should have joy too. It seemed to me that they should have even *more* joy, if they had known Jesus the longest amount of time. I had only known Him a few weeks and I was thrilled.

In those early days we sang a very simple song, written by Lynn DeShazo. It became one of the most beautiful things I had ever heard. I learned to worship Jesus through this one song, and loved watching the happy song leader sing it with all of his heart.

THE FADE

"Lord, You are, more precious than silver.
Lord, You are, more costly than gold.
Lord, You are, more beautiful than diamonds.
Nothing I desire compares with You."

No matter what difficult thing was happening on any given day, if I made my way to that little brick building and we found ourselves singing that song, my spirit was restored, and joy would flood my heart! The warmth of God's presence and the feelings of His love and acceptance became my hiding place. To this day, when I read the words "secret place" in scripture, I think of those times of worship. It was all anchored in *joy*. I was just so happy to be loved, forgiven, and have Jesus!

Step forward a couple of years and I came home to visit. I had become a very serious *church person* in the town we had moved to. My wife and I rarely missed anything. Two times on Sunday. Bible study Wednesday night. Sunday school before morning church. Men's Bible study in someone's home. We were always doing something faith-related, and we knew far more scripture than we had when that simple song so moved me. The morning I returned, my heart was nostalgic when the piano began to play that song. It was like stepping into the past. Everything was the same because nothing in that little church had changed; same piano and same pews, same pulpit and same overhead projector, same happy man singing to his Savior behind the familiar looking pulpit. One thing was very different: me. It took a few repeated choruses for me to realize that the *joy* was gone. I closed my eyes even tighter and really tried to focus, but the truth was unavoidable the longer I sang along. All I was doing was singing along. The *joy* of knowing Christ, and those simple lyrics being the truth of my life, had vanished. What was wrong with me?

It is possible that as you read this you can relate. As we have skimmed through the topic of joy and its ever-diminishing quality in our lives, you may be realizing that you have experienced that too. Has your joy in Christ faded? When you think back to the wonder and amazement that filled your heart when you first came to faith, can you confidently say you have retained it? Or has knowing Jesus as your Savior faded in beauty like the car, the house, the job, and the family that used to fill your heart with happiness?

Paul realized there was *another power* working inside us that was contrary to all the goodness of the Kingdom of God.

I began to realize, to my dismay, that it had managed to corrupt my faith on some level, and I no longer was genuinely *joyful* in knowing Jesus. I was serious, committed, and learning, but I was no longer happy about it. I am grateful that standing before me was this *happy man* who had managed to stay that way for years and years as he served Jesus. I did not know how he managed it, but I left that little building that morning determined to find out. Somehow, Jesus gave victory over the rotting influence of sin and flesh, and my intention was to pursue Him for the answer and the joy.

Everything I am about to share with you is what I learned on that journey.

THE FADE

Let me encourage you from the beginning to avoid the emotional traps of our modern day. Far too many turn every assertion into a confrontation. "If you say we can always be joyful, you might offend someone unhappy right now." That is a possibility. I am willing to risk it to share the pathway to restored happiness and joy. Far too often we choose to settle for less and then expect affirmation of that choice. Jesus is the One Who said we could be full of joy. I will listen to Him. I hope you do as well.

As we journey through the chapters of this book, moments of reflection will guide you toward deeper understanding and connection with Christ. The questions at the end of each section are designed to help you pause, ponder, and honestly assess where you stand in your walk with Him. They are not meant to challenge your faith but to rekindle the joy that may have faded and illuminate areas where His light can shine brighter. Take your time with these questions, allowing them to lead you into prayerful conversations with Jesus, where true transformation begins.

Before continuing, please take a moment to reflect on the following questions, which are designed to help you consider your journey and begin reconnecting with the joy of knowing Christ.

AMAZED AGAIN

INTRODUCTION REFLECTION QUESTIONS

"What happened to my joy?"

1. When you think back to your own salvation experience, what emotions do you remember being most notable and inspiring?
2. Can you recall how those early feelings impacted your life and your relationships?
3. Do you think your early church experiences built you up and increased your joy and satisfaction in knowing Christ? And if not, can you remember specific occurrences that had a negative impact?
4. How has the "other power" Paul speaks of worked against your desires and commitments to serve Jesus?
5. In what areas of your faith journey has a relationship with your church managed to replace your personal relationship with Christ?
6. If you stopped all involvement with an organized church, how would you be able to describe your relationship with Christ? How much of your personal time would be spent in fellowship with Him?

―――

"But if you possess faith, your heart cannot do otherwise than laugh for joy in God, and grow free, confident and courageous. For how can the heart remain sorrowful and dejected when it entertains no doubt of God's kindness to it, and of his attitude as a good friend with whom it may unreservedly and freely enjoy all things?"

—Martin Luther

CHAPTER ONE

THE BEGINNING

There was so much joy at the beginning. Do you remember? One of my favorite things to hear when talking with other believers is their story of salvation and coming to faith in Christ. The variety of ways that the Lord works to bring the Gospel message into broken lives is truly remarkable. It is always personal and fueled by this amazing love that our God has for the whole word. One of the most interesting aspects of every retelling is the emotion in the story. For some it still moves them in a very deep place. They smile, or their eyes moisten, and the words are inspiring. For others it is mechanical and logical and honestly, not very moving at all. How do we lose the joy of salvation? More importantly, how do we get it back?

> "When they came up out of the water, the Spirit of the Lord snatched Philip away. The eunuch never saw him again but went on his way rejoicing."
>
> *Acts of the Apostles 8:39 NLT*

This account from Acts contains all of the powerful elements. The Holy Spirit literally moves Philip into position and he shares the Gospel with this Ethiopian man. After coming to faith, the man asks to be baptized as a testimony to his new life in Christ. Philip baptized him and the man went on his way rejoicing.

Historically speaking, the Gospel then makes its way into a whole new part of the ancient world through this precious Ethiopian man. For those of us born again, our own story contains the same elements, even if they seem less dramatic.

We all have encountered at least one witness, like Philip the Evangelist, who was willing to share Christ with us.

Most of us heard the good news from multiple sources before we turned our lives to Christ and His Kingdom. In the encounter we are looking at in the book of Acts, the Holy Spirit tangibly orchestrated the entire encounter. We see God moving toward the lost man when so many would have us believe God is simply waiting for us to figure things out on our own. His love keeps the Church and the Gospel moving forward into this world. Whether you and I realize it or not, the same Holy Spirit was working to bring us the message of Christ.

"For no one can come to me unless the Father who sent me draws them to me, and at the last day I will raise them up."

John 6:44 NLT

THE BEGINNING

"But how can they call on him to save them unless they believe in him? And how can they believe in him if they have never heard about him? And how can they hear about him unless someone tells them? And how will anyone go and tell them without being sent? That is why the Scriptures say, 'How beautiful are the feet of the messengers who bring good news!'"

Romans 10:14-15 NLT

The people who told you and I about Jesus were sent to us by God Himself! The implications of this are life-changing when you take a moment and think about it. It means salvation came to us, from a loving God, Who wanted to redeem us from our sins so that we could walk in new life. We are wanted. We are chosen. We have value in our Creator's eyes. We do not find Him, but rather, we realize that He is coming into the darkness to find us!

Think back for a minute and remember who told you about Jesus. When you get that firmly in your mind, take another minute and thank God for sending that person to you. Man or woman, friend or stranger, for you they became Philip the Evangelist. Jesus was revealing Himself to us through them.

> **In my life, it was a three-step plan, but I'm also very confident there were a lot of other steps I did not realize God was taking toward me.**

My mother was first. She was the first person in our family to follow Jesus. She accepted Christ at a Baptist revival she had been invited to by a coworker. My father was not very pleased about it, but she did not appear to care about that very much. My brother and I did not understand it, but she was very happy with the decision. She was always reading her Bible. And one day I was shocked to find her writing in it! I knew nothing about God, but I was sure it must be a sin to underline verses with a red pencil the way she was. She never missed church. About one time per month, she would try and make us go with her. Most often our father did not support her in this effort and we were able to make excuses and worm our way out of it. Occasionally, after poor decision-making that had led to disciplinary action, he would make us go with her. Church never really moved me, but the words she told me before she died of cancer when I was fifteen years old did. Her final words to me are too personal to share, but they were a challenge to find Jesus, hang on to Him, and follow Him so she would see me again. They have never left me.

The second person was a neighborhood friend of mine. We had known each other since the first grade. His family were all Christians and attended church very regularly. By high school, we had different interests, but we were still friends. When he saw me spiraling out of control after my mom's death, he started bugging me. If you had asked me at the time if the Holy Spirit was sending me a lifeline, I would have said no, my old friend is just being a pain. Now I know it was a lifeline. I rejected his invitations to his youth group dozens of times. I laughed when he invited me to his church. I resented his mother asking me how I was doing when my own mother was gone. He just persisted and kept asking me.

THE BEGINNING

We started to spend more time together than we had the previous couple of years, and he kept asking. And I kept saying no. Somebody was probably praying for me because one day I accepted his invitation to a youth meeting before I could stop myself! I couldn't believe the words coming out of my own mouth. "Sure, what time does it start?" I was very disappointed in myself.

In short order, this led me to my third person. He was a young and excited youth evangelist of some kind. I had no church background to define what was happening so I cannot be more specific. It was a youth meeting with kids from several different towns in our state. They sang for a while, and then a strange guy acted out a song that was playing. Everyone around me seemed very moved by it all but I did not follow what was happening. The beginning of the young minister's message signaled to me that it was almost over and that was a relief. All I had to do was sit and listen for a few minutes and then we would be on our way. That is when everything went sideways for me. It was like he was talking directly to me. Every word seemed to be hard to ignore. When he was closing out his talk, he stopped and said the Holy Spirit was showing him a troubled young man that Jesus was there to save. He then proceeded to tell my entire story without knowing me at all! It was so precise that it left me confused because I could think of no possible way for this guy to know the things he knew. By the time we were driving home, I was a new creation in Christ.

That was how it all started. And very much like the Ethiopian gentleman in our Bible text, I went on my way rejoicing. The joy I had in my heart was remarkable. Is your journey like that at all? If you are a follower of Jesus, the elements are there even if the specifics are completely different. You were witnessed to. Someone—led by the Lord Himself—shared with you the most powerful message of hope ever entrusted to mankind; the Gospel of Jesus Christ. In some setting or another, you accepted Jesus as your Savior. Your prayer was probably different than mine, but if you are following Him today, it is because He heard you and forgave you. He did the same for me. He wiped away all of our sin! With the weight and stain gone, joy came in and we knew we were children of God.

For me, those early days were simple to sum up. My friend folded me into his youth group and his youth leaders folded me into their family. The pastor of his little church looked me up and down with a little suspicion (warranted by my appearance and attitude) and then folded me into his church. My father had found a new love and had moved on emotionally. We saw each other every day, but there was no connection anymore. In these strange church people, I found a new family. There was not much school left, and then I was going to be leaving for the Navy, but all of them showed me and taught me everything they could about following Jesus in the time we had. I was happy. Jesus had delivered me from a lot of darkness and with His light in my heart, I was happy. I had a lot of questions but those who I asked would smile and pull a Bible out and show me the truth. When I messed up, they would correct me. By the time I left, I had a good foundation of faith built into my heart.

THE BEGINNING

As I searched for the keys to reclaim my joy, I realized that joy was already returning as I remembered God's faithfulness in reaching out to me until I found my way back to Him.

I am wanted by God! That is an amazing thing that I had lost sight of in the routines of serving in my church. He chose me to be His son. He did not consider His family to be complete without me being part of it. Have you thought about that lately? He feels the same way about you. Your faith beginning was authored by Him. He was the One working behind the scenes and it was all motivated by His love for you. You are wanted and chosen too! Take some time and look back to your beginning. Ask the Lord to help you see His hand and His Spirit working in bringing you to Christ. I will not be surprised if this beginning step starts to rekindle some of your joy in knowing Christ as well.

AMAZED AGAIN

CHAPTER ONE REFLECTION QUESTIONS

"It was there when I started."

1. Who first told you about Christ, and what circumstances led to that conversation?

2. What do you remember about the span of time between learning about Christ and His sacrifice and personally accepting Him as your Savior?

3. When you look back at the beginning of your faith journey, what specific actions can you list that were clearly God reaching toward you? Where do you see His hand in you coming to saving faith?

4. How does the thought that God wants you in His family and pursues you until you are His affect your mindset?

5. Can you think of areas in your life where you have reacted more like an orphan than an adopted and beloved child?

"It is the consciousness of the threefold joy of the Lord, His joy in ransoming us, His joy in dwelling within us as our Saviour and Power for fruitbearing and His joy in possessing us, as His Bride and His delight; it is the consciousness of this joy which is our real strength. Our joy in Him may be a fluctuating thing: His joy in us knows no change."

—James Hudson Taylor

CHAPTER TWO

THE SOURCE

The declaration that Jesus would be the source of joy for all humanity was made even before He spoke a single word. Long before He performed miracles or delivered stirring teachings about the Kingdom of God, the messengers of Heaven proclaimed that He would bring us joy.

". . . but the angel reassured them. 'Don't be afraid!' he said. 'I bring you good news that will bring joy to all people.'"

Luke 2:10 NLT

Within the person of Jesus, we find the source of joy. The announcement of His birth carries the promise of joy to all who encounter Him. That promise is actually stunning when you consider how difficult it is to get any group of people to agree about anything in this world. We divide into our camps and tribes over almost every possible preference and opinion. Rarely will even a small group of people meeting for a shared purpose actually agree on everything. Yet in Christ, the angel announces a source of joy for *all people*. How can this be? The simple answer is found in Who He is declared to be.

"The Savior—yes, the Messiah, the Lord—has been born today in Bethlehem, the city of David!"

Luke 2:11 NLT

That is one power-packed statement. If we investigate it briefly, the possibility of joy for all people comes into focus. We do have to try and see it from the perspective of Jewish individuals alive at that time to fully appreciate the magnitude of it. An exhaustive work could be done on this topic alone, but we will look into it briefly on our way to the rest of our learning.

When the angel announces the Messiah is born, we must first apprehend the fact that to any Israelite it meant *The Promise* that God had been making since the very beginning of their existence was finally coming to pass. Many sectors of the Christian church await the second coming of Christ, or the rapture of the church, as they study end-time events. The announcement of the Messiah's birth would be equal to the sounding of the trumpet of God when Christ returns to earth. Every promise memorized and then repeated pointed to the day when God's chosen servant, the Messiah, would come and bring freedom to their nation. Every honored and venerated Old Testament prophet had declared this wonderful news. On every Sabbath in every synagogue, it was announced as the source of their hope. God was finally keeping His promise and the Deliverer of Israel was born!

THE SOURCE

If that was the full scope of the situation, it would limit this joy spoken of by the angels to only the Jewish people. We have the benefit of history, and we know that one of the primary sources of the bitter disappointment Jewish people had with Jesus was that He did not overthrow their oppressors and set them free. They were waiting for their Messiah to bring them a political victory that would restore their national prosperity and pride. Christ instead arrived to wage war on the power of sin and forever break its hold on *everyone* who would believe Him. This victory was wider in scope than just the children of Abraham. He would make victory and eternal life available to all the people, just as the angels announced.

> *"After all, is God the God of the Jews only? Isn't he also the God of the Gentiles? Of course he is. There is only one God, and he makes people right with himself only by faith, whether they are Jews or Gentiles."*
>
> Romans 3:29-30 NLT

When we experience the power of salvation, we find joy. Our salvation is our deliverance from sin and the death made inevitable by sin. With salvation being offered to *all people* by the power of personal faith in Christ, the joy of that salvation is available to *all people*.

> *"You love him even though you have never seen him. Though you do not see him now, you trust him; and you rejoice with a glorious, inexpressible joy."*
>
> 1 Peter 1:8 NLT

The angel added one additional detail that we will pause and remember. He declared the Messiah to be the Lord. In our Western cultures, the word *lord* seems to lack impact as more time passes. We often sing beautiful songs that celebrate the fact that Jesus is *Lord* and still not comprehend what that statement truly means for all of us. To the first-century audience, this statement carried a tremendous amount of weight. To call the Messiah the *Lord*, was to declare His supremacy over every other power or authority. It is one thing for someone to tell you a deliverer is coming to help you. That causes joy. It is propelled to a whole new level when the same person can inform you that the deliverer coming for you is more powerful than any other authority on this planet. The news that no power can stand against Him, and that every person He sets out to deliver will find freedom—because no one can stop Him—fills us with a reason to shout. Or at least it should. This power is proven by the resurrection of Jesus from the dead and His ascension to the right hand of God.

Jesus our Lord, the Messiah of God, is the source of joy for *all people* because, in Him, *all people* can find freedom and eternal life. This is such good news that it should be impossible for any of us who believe it and have tasted how sweet forgiveness is to ever lose our joy. As Peter said, it should be *a glorious and inexpressible joy* within every single believer. He literally means that we should be so joyful that it takes away our words. Far too often we find ourselves being silent in our service to Jesus, not because joy has surged in our hearts and interrupted our words, but because we have lost our joy and are simply no longer saying anything about it. My brothers and sisters, this should not be.

THE SOURCE

When I realized that the salvation I had experienced— that had changed the entire trajectory of my life— was no longer inspiring joy, I was truly alarmed.

Two primary thoughts caused my shock: The first one was that my joy had faded so slowly that I had not noticed it was gone. The second was that Jesus does not change and that meant that my lack of joy was 100% a heart problem within me. He is my Savior. He is the fulfillment of God's promise to deliver us. He is full of power and authority. He had washed my heart clean as the new falling snow when I had prayed and asked Him to forgive me. He had surrounded me with a new family that had loved me and taught me His ways. In my case, He had gone another step and brought salvation to the person I loved with all my heart. We had gotten married and we were living together as followers of Jesus. I simply had no reason to resign my joy and allow it to fail within me.

The same Savior announced that wonderous night by those angels is living inside the life of every truly born-again believer. That was the strength of His promise to all of us.

> *"For God wanted them to know that the riches and glory of Christ are for you Gentiles, too. And this is the secret: Christ lives in you. This gives you assurance of sharing his glory."*
>
> *Colossians 1:27 NLT*

What the Christian has in Christ goes far beyond a new worldview or a new perspective on life. Our faith takes us to a place that eclipses mere intellect and reason. Jesus is not a new religious preference that helps people look outside of themselves and see the universe in a new light. He is more than a pathway to some form of spiritual plurality that is so popular today. He is not a concept and He is not contained within a creed. He is God's only Son. He is our Savior and Messiah. He is the absolute Lord and King over all. He is eternal in power and authority. He makes His home, by His Spirit, within every believer. Only in Christianity does a person's God and Creator come and live inside of them. His indwelling presence becomes the actual line of demarcation between those who truly know Him and those who do not.

"But you are not controlled by your sinful nature. You are controlled by the Spirit if you have the Spirit of God living in you. (And remember that those who do not have the Spirit of Christ living in them do not belong to him at all.)"

Romans 8:9 NLT

When I looked back to my beginning with Christ, I was reminded that the joy that entered into my heart was Jesus Himself. I think we often reference that experience as just relief, or the lifting of burdens, or finding our freedom in Christ. While all of those descriptions are accurate to a degree, we cannot afford to overlook the greater truth taught in Scripture. Jesus moves into our hearts. He is making a new home within us when we receive Him and He brings joy with Him. Let that sink in for a second. The joy we feel when we come to faith is not just a feeling. That joy is the reality of a *Person*. Jesus brings joy with Him into our darkened hearts.

THE SOURCE

When I realized that, a very well-known scripture suddenly made a lot more sense to me.

"And Nehemiah continued, 'Go and celebrate a feast of rich foods and sweet drinks, and share gifts of food with people who have nothing prepared. This is a sacred day before our Lord. Don't be dejected and sad, for the joy of the Lord is your strength!'"

Nehemiah 8:10 NLT

For the believer in Christ, this statement by Nehemiah should take on a whole new life and scope. In the Old Testament, Nehemiah declares that God's joy at His people returning to the land should give them strength. In essence, he is saying, "Throw this party and celebrate because our God is celebrating with you!" God is rejoicing over what is happening on the earth because it pleases Him and represents restoration for His chosen people. Can you see the difference on this side of the cross of Christ? Our restoration is now eternal. Our redemption now includes freedom from the power of death. Our salvation delivers us from the power of darkness and restores us to fellowship with our Heavenly Father. We are now the children of God. Jesus Himself comes and makes a new home within us as He resurrects our dead spirit from the grip of sin. Now the *joy of the Lord* is more than an idea.

The *joy of the Lord* is literally within us because the Lord is literally within us with His joy.

With all of this wonderful news, I was still left pondering the original question: how did my joy in knowing Jesus fade away? In light of this perspective, I was actually more disturbed for a while. If Jesus lives inside of me, how is it even possible that I would lose my joy? The more I pored through the scripture, the more the happy guy leading the songs at my old church made perfect sense. All of us who had lost our smile seemed the ones in decline and in trouble. I was encouraged that if Jesus has joy over me, and He lives inside of me, it was not a long journey to getting back in touch with His joy. It reminded me of an old advertisement for a popular spaghetti sauce. The slogan was "It's in there." Do you remember that one? I found myself looking deeper inside the non-smiling guy in my mirror and reminding him that the joy of the Lord is in there. Somewhere.

THE SOURCE

CHAPTER TWO REFLECTION QUESTIONS

"How does anyone with Christ lose their joy?"

1. When you read the phrase "the joy of the Lord," what do you picture as the source of that joy?
2. As Christians, why do you think it is easy for us to lose our focus on the fact that Christ is living inside of us?
3. If someone asked you to explain how you know the Holy Spirit is within you, what would you point to as the evidence of His presence?
4. In what ways can reflecting on God's faithfulness to keep His promises reignite our joy in knowing Him?
5. Paul calls Christ dwelling within us the "hope of sharing in His glory." What are the personal implications of Jesus truly living within you?

"Therefore, we discover joy when we discover truth—the truth about God our Father, the truth about Jesus our Savior, the truth about the Holy Spirit who lives in our hearts."

—Saint Pope John Paul II

CHAPTER THREE

THE WORD

"When I discovered your words, I devoured them. They are my joy and my heart's delight, for I bear your name, O Lord God of Heaven's Armies."

Jeremiah 15:16 NLT

My quest to rediscover my joy in Christ was causing me to search His Word for the answers. What I noticed was that even before I had all my answers, I was recognizing more of my old joy starting to rise within my heart. I was not back to new-believer happy, but I was rejoicing more and it was reaching to my face. What I was finding in the Bible, some of which I have shared so far with you, was breathing new life on the embers in my soul. The more I meditated on these things, and the more I was bringing them into my times of prayer, the more they were becoming *my joy and heart's delight* as Jeremiah said in the scripture above. This was reviving me in wonderful ways, but it was also increasing my desire to find even more pillars of truth I could use to anchor my faith. I really did want to find a way to be that happy singing guy if I could.

This journey took time. This journey took a *long* time. Each time, I found another piece of my joy puzzle that would carry me a good distance. Then a new challenge or another life transition would happen, and my joy in Christ would be diluted again. I could feel it fade and that, in turn, would send me back to the Word. We never go wrong searching the scriptures. That will always lead us to strength and more clarity. Over my many years of ministry, I still find it puzzling how few Christians are truly students of the scriptures. All the answers are there.

"I rejoice in your word like one who discovers a great treasure."

Psalms 119:162 NLT

Take a minute and think about what we have talked about so far. It is all like treasure. Jesus is the One Who frees us from the influence of death and the hidden power that works within us, which we looked at in the first chapter. He said that He wanted us to have His joy within us and that He desired for us to be full of joy. Then we took a look back to reacquire our memories of the beginning of our faith journey—the joy we found in Jesus at the start. The Scripture helps us see the amazing truth that the Lord Himself led whoever shared the Gospel with us. He wanted us to be in His family and brought us the pathway out of the darkness. Then we just examined the fact that Christ Himself is living inside of us as believers and He brings the joy of the Lord with Him. The Savior the angels were shouting about outside

THE WORD

of Bethlehem is now living inside of each and every redeemed child of God! All of this feels like very valuable and precious treasure to me. We find all of it, and more, in the pages of the Bible.

If you have managed to follow my story to this point, we have arrived at something important for all Christians to comprehend. As I mentioned, the morning I realized my joy had somehow gone missing, I was very active in my church and constantly being taught the Bible. Our entire week was scheduled around church in those days. We took notes during sermons. We attended various Bible studies. My wife and I sometimes relaxed at home watching even more preaching via videotapes. (I just gave away my age.) There was no shortage of us listening to people teach us about what was in the Bible. Without exaggeration, I would guess that five or six hours of every week we were listening to Biblical presentations of one form or another. If we can find joy in hearing preaching about Scripture, then we should have been overflowing in happiness. If we find joy in the teaching of Scripture, everyone should leave every church this coming Sunday with a goofy grin and the joy of the Lord glowing in their heart. We all know that will not be the case. This caused me to discover a life-changing truth.

There is a world of difference between *listening* to someone tell me what is in the Bible and *receiving* from the Holy Spirit what He is revealing about what is in the Bible.

AMAZED AGAIN

Have you ever noticed what the gospels tell us about how people reacted to the teachings of Jesus?

"There, too, the people were amazed at his teaching, for he spoke with authority."

Luke 4:32 NLT

"He returned to Nazareth, his hometown. When he taught there in the synagogue, everyone was amazed and said, 'Where does he get this wisdom . . . ?'"

Matthew 13:54 NLT

"When the crowds heard him, they were astounded at his teaching."

Matthew 22:33 NLT

Jesus was so powerful in His presentation of Kingdom truth that even complete enemies were amazed by Him:

"When the Temple guards returned without having arrested Jesus, the leading priests and Pharisees demanded, 'Why didn't you bring him in?' 'We have never heard anyone speak like this!' the guards responded."

John 7:45-46 NLT

When Jesus was speaking, it impacted everyone who heard it. He either inspired hope and joy or offense and anger, but nobody ignored Him. His words had the weight of Heaven behind them and even people who did not believe anything about Him could feel that. He brought conviction

THE WORD

of sin to many with just His words. He brought hope and faith to many others with just His words. Just by talking, He calmed storms and raised the dead. The consistent observation in the gospels is that people were amazed by His instruction. When we consider the context of these encounters, it is interesting to notice that this amazement was felt by people who attended synagogue routinely and were often under the instruction of the scribes and Pharisees. These are people who regularly heard people tell them what God had said historically but they were now hearing God Himself say things to them personally. It made all the difference.

Why was my personal study bringing me so much more joy than the corporate church learning environment? It did not require much analysis to figure out why. It was the same source material, the Bible. It was the same basic topical constructions: Jesus, redemption, forgiveness, etc. It was even the same pair of ears connected to the same brain! It was me, in both settings. Yet the personal study was bringing life to my very soul and the group study setting was apparently filling my head with information that was not reaching beyond the cerebral realms. The disconnect was within me somewhere because Jesus was talking to groups when they walked away and said He was amazing. What follows requires some careful consideration, and I really need you to follow me until the end, without falling into some of the same flawed conclusions I did early on.

My first flawed conclusion about all of this was that it was my pastor's fault. That had to be it. He was simply not an amazing teacher like Jesus and what I must need to reclaim my joy was better preaching. It was the classic sentiment of "this is not feeding me." This was before the internet made browsing for other speakers so much easier. I embraced listening to teachings on cassette tapes in my car. That in itself was not a problem except my heart attitude about it was definitely off base. I felt inspired listening to great sermons in my car, but when I attended our local church services, I was often bored and just went through the motions to keep up appearances. Looking back, it saddens me to think how many times I was in a room with someone teaching and the entire time I was thinking about a different message I had listened to earlier and thought was better. It was unfair to the minister in front of me, and it revealed a very immature attitude on my part.

It is possible that as you are reading this, parts of it are hitting home for you. Are you sitting through the ministry offerings at your church with no expectation that what is shared can truly feed you? Maybe you have become very well versed in which corner of YouTube you can surf through and find what you like better. In this age of high-profile ministries that consistently make what appear to be perfect presentations, it is not difficult for most of us to find something online that looks and sounds better than what our local fellowship can muster up. If you find yourself there, one of the most deceptive aspects of it is that you feel superior about it. Somewhere in our hearts, we entertain the idea that we are deeper and somehow more serious about following Jesus. We then conclude our local offering of Christian basics is just not good enough for us. We often do not say it out loud, or at least not to everyone, but we hold the attitude within our

THE WORD

hearts. Instead of this conclusion, consider that it may be our own attitudes that stand in our way.

The next false conclusion I gravitated toward was that it might be better to just not belong to a church. My logic was this: If Jesus and I can have a wonderful relationship, and I can grow in that relationship with my personal devotions, then why do I need the hassle of going to a church? Once I opened the door to that stream of thought, it rapidly picked up speed. I could give my money to the poor, instead of funding this big expense of the church building and the staff salaries. I would not have to worry about being judged for what I was doing because all of the judgmental people would still be in church. We would not have to waste time and money on nice clothes for Sunday because we would not be trying to fit in with all these religious people. Best of all, no more sitting through boring sermons that were not deep enough to feed me anyway. It sounded great! The absence of hypocrites, who obviously all go to church, was just a bonus.

Fortunately for me, we were too involved in our local church to just pull the ejection handle and vanish. That gave me time to think about it all and pray. Some pesky Bible verses were in the way of my escape plan.

> "And let us not neglect our meeting together, as some people do, but encourage one another, especially now that the day of his return is drawing near."
>
> *Hebrews 10:25 NLT*

> *"I am writing to Philemon, our beloved co-worker, and to our sister Apphia, and to our fellow soldier Archippus, and to the church that meets in your house."*
>
> Philemon 1:1-2 NLT

Then there was the broader observation that Jesus, and then the apostles of the Lord, had certainly invested a lot, often their lives, into the establishment of the Church. In every corner of the Earth, in every century since the upper room, the Church had always gathered together. I started to feel pretty silly concluding that Jesus was doing such a great work in my life that I was going to abandon the entity that He established. The Holy Spirit began to deal with me about the idea that I was just too deep to be a part of the modern church. Jesus loves His Church, and if I love Him, retreating from what He loves and established Himself, felt like a betrayal. Then I realized that I was already attending church and having great personal devotions with Christ, and so the issue wasn't the church itself but my own pride. I was using the flaws I perceived in the church as an excuse to disengage, rather than seeking how I could contribute to its growth and healing. Instead of abandoning the body of believers, the Holy Spirit was showing me that I needed to lean in—not to consume but to serve.

The final flawed idea that I entertained was more fatalistic. Maybe church was never going to feed me or result in any joy in my life. Maybe church was just the place of duty and service where we help younger believers discover all those basic doctrines and principles, and those of us a little further along in our journey should accept it as simply a place of

THE WORD

service. Jesus had certainly emphasized the idea of putting the needs of others first and focusing on being servants rather than being served. Maybe the mature attitude about my local church was to have dynamic times with Jesus at home, and feed myself, and then roll up my sleeves and find a place to serve at my local church while planning to get nothing much out of it. Several verses in the New Testament can actually support the case for this idea. Serving certainly sounded far more noble and Christ-like than blaming my pastor for my lack of joy, or running away into the woods and never attending anywhere again. Where the first two flawed ideas were relatively short-lived in my journey, this third one held on for quite a while.

"God has given each of you a gift from his great variety of spiritual gifts. Use them well to serve one another."

1 Peter 4:10 NLT

"Never be lazy, but work hard and serve the Lord enthusiastically."

Romans 12:11 NLT

With this idea safely resolved in my understanding, I set about serving Jesus. When I would pray and worship in my private time, it would fuel my life with the power of His Kingdom. When I did ministry at the church and served the Lord there, I had no expectation of receiving anything from it. If it was difficult or I was weary, I just accepted that and kept walking forward. When others would ask me why I kept serving in tough seasons, I would explain that Jesus and I were doing fine and I did not need easy times at the church to follow Him. This mindset removed all confusion, and if I saw a need, I moved to serve the Lord and meet that need because we are called to serve. When nothing about the church was bringing me any joy, I did not mind at all because early the following day Jesus and I were going to open His Word together and I would find my joy there. For all the ministry that this seemed to enable me to do, it was still falling short of the true answer to this dilemma. If Scripture is being taught at the church, then should it not be producing the same life-giving joy that I was finding in it when I was alone in my devotions with Jesus? After a long time living and serving with this mindset, I became the pastor. In this role, answering this question became important again.

Now there were people listening to me. The people were gathering and looking to be fed by my offerings. With all of my heart, I would preach the Kingdom of God to them at every opportunity. My fuel going into every message was the wonderful fellowship I was having with Jesus and the truth He was revealing to me. For all of my zeal and effort, I began to recognize the same vacant look on their faces that had adorned my own in my pre-pastoral years. How could this be? By God's grace, I am a fairly skilled communicator. I can construct a good sermon and deliver it well. I even know how to utilize humor and personal stories to keep it interesting. And yet, more often than not, the message that was burning in me seemed to fizzle in my audience. I would often receive compliments afterward: "That was a good message today brother." But the impact in them was not the same as the impact in me. The treasures I was sharing from

THE WORD

God's Word should be bringing them joy. What was wrong with me? What was wrong with them? I began to search and dig again.

In my new study, I found an amazing passage of scripture that seemed to describe the situation perfectly. During the days of the prophet Ezekiel, the people of God had been taken captive to another land because of their persistent sin. God, ever faithful, had provided them a voice even in that faraway place. It is amazing to realize that even when we wander, He continues to call to us. His invitation is always to come back home to Him and all can be restored. In His love for us, He also has perfect understanding of our hearts and it makes it impossible to fool Him. Listen to what He says to the Israelites in captivity through Ezekiel.

"Son of man, your people talk about you in their houses and whisper about you at their doors. They say to each other, 'Come on, let's go hear the prophet tell us what the Lord is saying!' So my people come pretending to be sincere and sit before you. They listen to your words, but they have no intention of doing what you say. Their mouths are full of lustful words, and their hearts seek only after money. You are very entertaining to them, like someone who sings love songs with a beautiful voice or plays fine music on an instrument. They hear what you say, but they don't act on it!"

Ezekiel 33:30-32 NLT

It is very possible you have never read that section before. It is also possible that as a modern church-goer, you feel the sting of it like everyone else who reads it with a tender heart.

Ministry is very entertaining now. Great amounts of energy and resources are invested to make sure it is the best show possible. Have we grown accustomed to watching the show and then leaving again with no intention of changing course or commitment? When the Lord speaks of lustful words, He is saying that their conversation is filled with all the things they want and desire rather than a concern for what He wants and desires as their God. Looking only for the next dollar, they were adjusting to life in a foreign country and seeking ways to turn the situation to their advantage rather than turning their hearts back to God. This is a brutally honest assessment of their heart condition! It is spoken in their faces as they sit in front of Ezekiel and play the part of being God's people while living entirely for themselves.

I can honestly tell you that this scripture really disturbed me. It caused me to closely examine my ministry and what I was bringing to the people. Was I focused on entertaining them? Was there a hidden part of my heart longing for a compliment and a pat on the back? In addition, it really made me pray about our church. The room was pretty full almost every Sunday but were they disciples seeking to follow Jesus or just Americans playing the part of being Christians while living for themselves? Many people never wrestle with these bigger questions because they are unpleasant and challenging, but let me encourage you to dive in. Search your own heart. Do you attend your church to be entertained and encouraged? Or are you seeking the truth of God so that you can be changed and truly transformed? Many today happily listen to sermons they agree with that have application to someone else and then turn away if the message hits home with them and confronts their mindsets and opinions. Was the vacant stare on the faces of many in our church simply a heart issue? Were all those times I had walked back to my car with the same vacant stare a heart issue in me?

The Scripture says a lot more to us about how we listen and receive the Word than it instructs those who are sharing it.

The more I investigated, the more it seemed that Jesus would say, "You don't need better preachers. You need better ears!" The very well-known parable of the sower certainly conveys this message. The *good seed* of the Word of the Kingdom was not the problem. The fruitfulness was determined by the conditions it found when it landed in the heart (soil). (See Luke chapter 8 to investigate further.) James made a very clear declaration about this in his short epistle to the Church.

"So get rid of all the filth and evil in your lives, and humbly accept the word God has planted in your hearts, for it has the power to save your souls. But don't just listen to God's word. You must do what it says. Otherwise, you are only fooling yourselves."

James 1:21-22 NLT

There are numerous applications to this, but maintaining our focus of finding joy, I began to really examine how I was listening. When I was having my personal devotions and searching God's Word prayerfully, was my heart more humble and willing to receive the message than when I was at church? If that was the case, then I needed to figure out *why*. In the process, if I could figure out how to listen better for myself, maybe I could also help my congregation learn the same lessons. We have more access to Biblical teaching today than any other generation of believers that has ever lived. Yet somehow, even though we are exposed to more seed, we are not bearing more fruit. We have a playlist of which ministries entertain us and make us feel good, but we are, generally speaking, not retaining and walking in those teachings. We desperately need to discover and repair this disconnect in our spiritual lives if we are to ever be what Jesus needs us to be. We must remember that one thing He desires us to walk in is the fullness of His joy! (John 15:11)

My attention was drawn back to the crowds listening to Jesus. They were consistently amazed and moved to radical change. On the surface, this observation was not very helpful because Jesus is not physically here to listen to. I was sure that all of us would be impacted by listening to Jesus preach. He is the Word of God after all. Our church ministries will always be a weak echo of our Savior. He alone was perfect. He alone was all-knowing. He alone walked in the full wisdom of God. He alone had perfect insight into every heart. He alone was fully God and fully man. None of us compare to Him on our very best day. Was that the answer? I was sure that it was. In my private times I was not listening to a ministry echo Jesus's teachings, I was listening to Jesus Himself! Through the ministry of the Holy Spirit, I was having fellowship directly with God. It was the same dynamic as the ancient audience listening to Jesus talking and then comparing it with the orations of the scribes at the synagogue. One is *life* and the other is information.

THE WORD

"*When the Spirit of truth comes, he will guide you into all truth. He will not speak on his own but will tell you what he has heard. He will tell you about the future. He will bring me glory by telling you whatever he receives from me. All that belongs to the Father is mine; this is why I said, 'The Spirit will tell you whatever he receives from me.'*"

John 16:13-15 NLT

"*But you have received the Holy Spirit, and he lives within you, so you don't need anyone to teach you what is true. For the Spirit teaches you everything you need to know, and what he teaches is true—it is not a lie. So just as he has taught you, remain in fellowship with Christ.*"

1 John 2:27 NLT

Life was found in what the Holy Spirit was teaching. It was the Spirit revealing truth inside that was releasing Kingdom joy. Paul alluded to this in his discussions of the Old and New Testaments.

"*He has enabled us to be ministers of his new covenant. This is a covenant not of written laws, but of the Spirit. The old written covenant ends in death; but under the new covenant, the Spirit gives life.*"

2 Corinthians 3:6 NLT

One older preacher I liked would call it the difference between *information* and *impartation*. The facts of the Scripture were information. The inner voice of the Author of the Scripture is impartation of everything good and eternal.

As the speaker most weekends, I was still wrestling with this question when the Lord led me to the last book in the Bible and gave me the answer.

In the book of Revelation, there are seven letters written to seven churches. In each letter, Jesus speaks and reveals His viewpoint of that particular church. He references their strengths and their weaknesses. He encourages them in their struggles and rebukes them in their sin. He brings His perspective to them so they can make any necessary changes to get into harmony with Him as the Lord of the Church. They are all different, but they all end the same way.

> "Anyone with ears to hear must listen to the Spirit and understand what he is saying to the churches."
>
> *Revelation 2:7 NLT*

In a very repetitive way, each letter ends with the same admonition. I did not have to be a scholar to realize that every believer, in every church, in every age, must be listening to what the Spirit is saying. Can you imagine getting a letter from the Apostle John in which he announces that Jesus Himself has sent a message to your church? You would gather the people and open your letter and read it together. What is Jesus saying to us? Then it would end with this command, "Listen to what the Spirit is saying to your church!" It then hit me like a load of bricks and changed everything about how I attended any church for the rest of my life.

The key was to listen for the Spirit speaking *through* whoever was speaking.

THE WORD

It was shocking to realize that in almost every church meeting, sermon, and teaching, I had been listening with the wrong ears. The fleshy ones on the sides of my head were hearing the words coming from the presenter but it had never occurred to me to listen deeper and *hear* what the Spirit was saying to me while they were talking. Because I was listening with my flesh ears, my observations were all natural and fleshy. I knew what stumbles had occurred and which scriptures had been misquoted. I knew it was too long and that it was not interesting enough. I could tell you almost everything about it, but was not listening to what the Spirit was saying *through* it. I had so limited the Spirit's role that I could not see His marvelous ability to speak no matter who was talking!

There is no exaggeration when I say that this changed everything. It also answered so many questions for me as a pastor. Why did one person leave our meeting moved to tears and changed, and the one sitting next to them was almost asleep? One of them had heard the voice of the Spirit coming to them through what was happening, and the other had only heard me talking. The person who had heard the Spirit speaking was filled with life. The person who had not heard the Spirit had only listened as I talked to them from the stage. I had never been taught how to listen when I was in church. It seemed safe to assume our congregation had not been instructed in this area either. When I was alone in my devotional times, there was nobody else to listen to. It was easy to listen for Him because we were alone. Somehow, in the church setting, I had been listening in the natural and only hearing what the other humans were saying.

If your joy has faded and attending your church is not doing much to resurrect it, take stock of how you listen when you are there. Listen for the voice of Jesus in the midst of what all His servants are doing. They mean well, but they are not Him. He is there and desires to bring you revelation in the midst of that meeting. Ask Him for the ears to hear what the Spirit is saying. Remember what Jesus told His disciples.

"The Spirit alone gives eternal life. Human effort accomplishes nothing. And the very words I have spoken to you are spirit and life."

John 6:63 NLT

My prayer, when I am the one speaking, is that the Lord will help each person truly hear what He is saying to them through what is happening. I encourage them to listen for His voice because it is more powerful than mine. Now when I am listening to someone else, I am listening for Him. I have found that this understanding transforms every gathering. I could tell you many stories of times the Lord has brought incredible and transformative truth to my soul while the person talking was not incredible or amazing. I have received Heaven-sent instruction when listening to the third chair fill-in-guy who forgot he was the one filling in that day. Jesus has revealed truth in my heart through the voices of children and elderly alike. Through their words, He has illuminated some aspect of His Word, and brought joy once again. That illuminated Word is like treasure and restores joy and delight. Listen for His voice when you are alone with Him and when you are gathered with the others, and let your joy rise as the Word of God *to you* brings the reality of eternal life into your soul!

THE WORD

CHAPTER THREE REFLECTION QUESTIONS

"The Word of God holds all the answers."

1. With the Scriptures declared to be God's word to all of us, why do you think we so often neglect to study them?
2. Can you list three (3) common daily occurrences that you could adjust and find more time to study the Bible?
3. What do you think makes the difference between just reading the Scripture and truly absorbing it and growing from that?
4. When it comes to our personal devotions, how important is our willingness to invest the necessary time?
5. If someone important to you asked you to meet with them daily, what adjustments would you be willing to make to your life to be faithful to that meeting?

"Joy is the serious business of heaven."

—C.S. Lewis

CHAPTER FOUR

THE KINGDOM

"You will show me the way of life, granting me the joy of your presence and the pleasures of living with you forever."

Psalms 16:11 NLT

"For the Kingdom of God is not a matter of what we eat or drink, but of living a life of goodness and peace and joy in the Holy Spirit."

Romans 14:17 NLT

One of the most neglected New Testament doctrines in the modern church, particularly in the West, is the Kingdom of God. A huge segment of the church world hears those words and simply thinks of Heaven or our eternal home after we die. Some smaller camps, mostly charismatic varieties, teach about the Kingdom but, unfortunately, often stray into areas of self-service and manipulation. I spent many years faithfully believing in Jesus and serving without understanding much about it. Thankfully, the reality of the Kingdom is not based on our understanding. We discover it, and once we do, it becomes the foundation of our life in Christ. We will not be exhaustive about it here, but let me encourage you to study it.

The Kingdom of God was the central message of the New Testament from the very beginning.

John the Baptist revealed himself to the world, preaching the Kingdom (Matthew 3:1-2). When Jesus began to publicly preach, His message was the Kingdom (Matthew 4:17). When the disciples were sent out, it was the message entrusted to them (Matthew 10:7). The Kingdom was the foundation of the parables that Jesus taught. When Jesus responded to Pilate during the mock trial, His reference was the Kingdom (John 18:36). What did the resurrected Christ teach the new church about when He was risen? That is right: the Kingdom of God (Acts 1:3). If we find ourselves not knowing about the Kingdom, an examination of Scripture makes us feel like the only people who don't know.

The reality of the Kingdom of God is the anchor for New Testament language about Jesus. We call Him *Lord Jesus* because He is the King (1 Corinthians 16:23). *Lord* was the very first title the Apostle Paul used in reference to Him (Acts 26:15). The understanding and declaration of His lordship is the primary confession that leads us to our salvation (Romans 10:9). Many have tried to make that a simple formula to be recited, but Jesus did not see His position that way.

THE KINGDOM

> *"So why do you keep calling Me 'Lord, Lord!' when you don't do what I say?"*
>
> Luke 6:46 NLT

His clear expectation is that we will understand He is Lord and our belief in Him will cause us to yield to Him and serve Him as the subjects of His Kingdom. Many today really labor to divide and refute what they will refer to as *Lordship* salvation. They quote numerous passages about faith in Christ and rail against anyone who implies that the Lordship of Jesus is essential to salvation. The main problem with their line of reasoning is that every person in the Bible knew that believing in Jesus included belief in Who He is, and He is the King. If my life does not reflect a surrender and adjustment to that reality, it reveals I do not actually believe He is Who He declares Himself to be. It would be like telling people you are married but then not living like you have a spouse. It is the realignment of your priorities that tells the entire world you got married. In the same way, it is our decisions to *follow* Jesus that indicate we have truly found Him, and not merely repeated words of confession.

All of this is important because whether you realize it or not, all of us who have truly been born again are already living in God's Kingdom!

> *"For he has rescued us from the kingdom of darkness and transferred us into the Kingdom of his dear Son, . . ."*
>
> Colossians 1:13 NLT

For as deep as some scholars try to make it, there is a simple truth.

AMAZED AGAIN

Every person who has surrendered and accepted Christ as their King is given a place in His Kingdom.

Our understanding of that grows and matures. None of us perfectly follow Him and all of us still battle with our old nature. Yet, the understanding of this transforms everything when it comes to Christian living. Christ is our King! It is why we obey His declarations. It is why we stand and give Him honor when we gather together for worship. It is why we minister and pray in His Name. It is why every mature believer submits to Christ whenever there is a conflict between what Jesus desires and what they desire. He is the One we are following. He is the One we are serving. He is the One we represent in this fallen world. He has granted us mercy and forgiveness from sin and allowed us to live in His Kingdom! Our response to this great gift is to serve Him faithfully and live for His purpose instead of our own. We are now citizens of His Kingdom.

"Above all, you must live as citizens of heaven, conducting yourselves in a manner worthy of the Good News about Christ."

Philippians 1:27 NLT

In our Romans passage referenced earlier, Paul teaches us that the reality of this Kingdom is revealed in a life of goodness, peace, and joy in the Holy Spirit. When someone walks past me on the street, they cannot see the flag of God's Kingdom with their natural eyes, but my life of goodness, peace, and joy reveals the reality of it within me. Paul contrasted this with those who tried to show and prove their

THE KINGDOM

godliness by performing their religious duties and rituals perfectly. By the Spirit, the believer in Jesus carries His Kingdom within, and the influence of it shines out in goodness, peace, and joy. As citizens of this Kingdom, part of our family trust and inheritance is to walk in goodness, peace, and joy. Get comfortable with the idea that all three of these virtues should be tangibly yours, each and every day.

Goodness in most Bible translations is referenced as *righteousness*, doing things that are God-like and right by His definition. The inner working power of God's goodness is why so many things about our lives change after we meet Jesus. We begin to act differently and display different priorities because what is good to Him starts being what we define as good in our own lives. Sometimes our desire to do what is good increases so rapidly that it shocks people who have known us for a while. To obey the Lord and walk in the good ways of God becomes more important than satisfying the appetites and whims of our old nature.

"For God is working in you, giving you the desire and the power to do what pleases him."

Philippians 2:13 NLT

The *peace* of the Kingdom goes a little deeper than just the feeling of peace. This peace is born out of the fact that the conflict with King Jesus is over. We have surrendered to His reign and therefore have peace with God. As those who have bowed before Him now, we have nothing to fear from Him later. He is our King. No matter what forms of judgment or trouble He visits upon His adversaries, we are no longer with them. We are with Him. We ride and march under His banner and our colors are His Kingdom. The armor we wear, we receive from Him (Ephesians 6). There are adversaries at war with Jesus and His ways, all around us. They are also at war with us. The war is the proof we are His soldiers. We only get attacked because we display His seal and ride behind His flag. Having peace with God and our eternal question answered, releases waves of peace into our souls.

"Then you will experience God's peace, which exceeds anything we can understand. His peace will guard your hearts and minds as you live in Christ Jesus."

Philippians 4:7 NLT

This brings us to our primary topic: the *joy* of the Kingdom. It would clearly follow that if I can walk in God's goodness and I can live in God's peace, I should also be a carrier of God's joy. It is declared as a proof of the Kingdom of God—right along with goodness and peace. The same inner power of His Spirit that works goodness and peace into my life is also working to bring joy. Our life experience helps us realize that just as our commitment to do what is right and good sometimes wavers, and trials and worries often buffet our peace in God, our joy also ebbs and flows. In the same way, we all know that if my goodness disappears entirely, something is very wrong in my spirit. If my peace is nowhere to be found, something has gone off the rails in my spirit. If my joy has vanished and been replaced with my somber Christian duty and a spirit of critical self-righteousness, something is just as wrong in my spirit. God fills us with the power of goodness, the reality of peace, and fullness of His joy!

Why would living surrendered to Jesus inspire joy? Our world teaches us that joy comes from getting things we want and obtaining goals we set. It tries to convince us that our entire happiness is found in realizing our dreams. How could we possibly find joy and fulfillment in giving all that away to live for someone else's desires and dreams? This conflict between the Kingdom of God and the kingdom of self is so stark that Paul utilizes the emergence of the kingdom of self as a warning sign for the last days.

> *"You should know this, Timothy, that in the last days there will be very difficult times. For people will love only themselves and their money. They will be boastful and proud, scoffing at God, disobedient to their parents, and ungrateful. They will consider nothing sacred."*
>
> *2 Timothy 3:1-2 NLT*

This deceptive attitude is so prevalent in our modern world that entire Christian ministries have been swallowed up in its influence. They announce with great charisma and boldness that Jesus is the One Who wants you to have all you desire. He is the One Who helps you make your dreams come true. Following Jesus is the path to abundance and trouble-free living, according to these salesmen. Those who consume this commodity know very little Scripture and are mostly unaware that Jesus *never* taught this. On the contrary, every book in the New Testament warned us about people who teach this. The Kingdom of God is about Jesus and what

He wants, not about what *we* want. The central figure in a Kingdom is the King, not the subjects who live there. The throne of this Kingdom is occupied by the Risen Christ and it leaves no place for us to serve ourselves.

The joy of the Kingdom of God is in realizing how *trustworthy* the God of the Kingdom truly is!

> *"I pray that God, the source of hope, will fill you completely with joy and peace because you trust in him. Then you will overflow with confident hope through the power of the Holy Spirit."*
>
> Romans 15:13 NLT

All the issues of this life that rob us of joy are confronted and conquered by the knowledge of the Kingdom. We worry about money and provision. Yet in a Kingdom, it is actually the King's responsibility to provide a way of life for His subjects. This is why Paul tells us to trust Him instead of ourselves.

> *"And this same God who takes care of me will supply all your needs from his glorious riches, which have been given to us in Christ Jesus."*
>
> Philippians 4:19 NLT

We work endlessly on our past and seek out therapy for comfort about everything that happened to us on our journey from birth to our rebirth in Jesus. We read and ponder and listen and rehearse in order to somehow process our past and take control of our futures. Regrets from the past rob us of joy. Yet in this Kingdom our past is no longer the issue.

THE KINGDOM

"Since you have been raised to new life with Christ, set your sights on the realities of heaven, where Christ sits in the place of honor at God's right hand. Think about the things of heaven, not the things of earth. For you died to this life, and your real life is hidden with Christ in God."

Colossians 3:1-3 NLT

"This means that anyone who belongs to Christ has become a new person. The old life is gone; a new life has begun!"

2 Corinthians 5:17 NLT

One of the greatest obstacles to joy for most is the uncertainty they feel about the future. What is going to happen? There is so much in the world that seems crazy and out of control. Our culture seems to be moving quickly in the wrong direction and so many of our leaders are corrupt and self-serving. How bad will things get? If things get really bad, what will we do? How will we make it through? Here again the Kingdom of God is the answer.

"This means that all of creation will be shaken and removed, so that only unshakable things will remain. Since we are receiving a Kingdom that is unshakable, let us be thankful and please God by worshiping him with holy fear and awe."

Hebrews 12:27-28 NLT

The book of Revelation was the final work of the Holy Spirit in releasing Scripture into the world. Most do not read this work because they find it confusing and scary. In avoiding it, they miss the point of it existing, and all the comfort they should find in the pages. It is scary and confusing because so often this world we live in seems scary and confusing. It is filled with imagery that is difficult to understand because we so often struggle to understand what we see around us. It speaks to spiritual realities that are awesome in scope because we are supposed to realize that the world we see is driven by a spiritual world the natural eye cannot see. What we should do is read it, often, and find the anchors for our souls. In the midst of all the passages that people debate and scholars dissect, some clear anchor points were designed by God to fill His Church with hope, peace and joy. The central theme is the Kingdom of God.

What was the revelation that Jesus sent to His people laboring and serving Him in an often chaotic world-system that was filled with trials and troubles? It was the wonderful news that He was still the King of the Kingdom!

"Then I heard again what sounded like the shout of a vast crowd or the roar of mighty ocean waves or the crash of loud thunder:

"Praise the Lord! For the Lord our God, the Almighty, reigns. Let us be glad and rejoice, and let us give honor to him. For the time has come for the wedding feast of the Lamb, and his bride has prepared herself."

Revelation 19:6-7 NLT

"Then I saw heaven opened, and a white horse was standing there. Its rider was named Faithful and True, for he judges fairly and wages a righteous war. His eyes were like flames of fire, and

on his head were many crowns. A name was written on him that no one understood except himself. He wore a robe dipped in blood, and his title was the Word of God. The armies of heaven, dressed in the finest of pure white linen, followed him on white horses. From his mouth came a sharp sword to strike down the nations. He will rule them with an iron rod. He will release the fierce wrath of God, the Almighty, like juice flowing from a winepress. On his robe at his thigh was written this title: King of all kings and Lord of all lords."

Revelation 19:11-16 NLT

"I, Jesus, have sent my angel to give you this message for the churches. I am both the source of David and the heir to his throne. I am the bright morning star."

Revelation 22:16 NLT

Do you see the theme? Do you sense the joy of it? Our King takes care of us now. Our King has redeemed us and washed away our past. Our King has given us new life and called us to a new path. Our King reigns forever, and no power or authority can challenge Him for His throne. Our King is the One Who will ultimately defend us and wage His war. Our King will overcome all adversaries and secure everlasting victory and peace. Our King is Jesus and He wears a robe dipped in blood that He shed to purchase our salvation! Heaven opens to reveal Him risen and reigning exactly where He promised He would be. Regardless of His timing, He renews His promise to come again and set things right. The entire work is declared by Jesus to be His special message to all of us so that we would not forget the throne is His. This is why the Kingdom of God is also *joy* in the Spirit.

CHAPTER FOUR REFLECTION QUESTIONS

"Living in the King's domain."

1. What words, phrases, or imagery would you use to describe the idea of a *kingdom* to someone else?

2. How long had you been serving Jesus before you learned that your faith in Him made you a citizen of His Kingdom? Where did you learn this?

3. What would you say are the tangible differences between a person saying that Jesus is Lord and a person surrendered to His lordship over them?

4. What qualities of life are taught as the outward signs, or the *flags* of God's Kingdom?

5. How is it helpful to remember that the presence of goodness, peace, and joy in our lives is an indicator of the health of our spirit?

6. What do you think is the most challenging part of realizing that in a Kingdom, the central figure is the King and not His subjects?

7. What specific aspect of having a Kingdom worldview begins to restore your joy in knowing Jesus?

"Joy, which was the small publicity of the pagan,
is the gigantic secret of the Christian."

—G.K. Chesterton

CHAPTER FIVE

THE FAMILY

One of the most fascinating parts of growing as a believer is an ever-expanding understanding of how wonderful our salvation is. We begin with simple faith and accept the Gospel as it is presented to us. From that day forward, if we are listening and open, the Holy Spirit begins to reveal one truth after another, little by little, one verse at a time, and our knowledge of Christ becomes greater and more complete. Every aspect we see should bring us joy.

"See how very much our Father loves us, for he calls us his children, and that is what we are! But the people who belong to this world don't recognize that we are God's children because they don't know him."

1 John 3:1 NLT

Well into my relationship with Christ, my wife and I watched a Christian concert. We have followed this artist's career from the very beginning, and we were excited to hear him singing his best songs, even if a video was as close as we could get to being there. One great tune after the next was delivered with conviction and energy. What really stood out was a moment in the middle of the concert when the band left the stage and he sat at a piano and began to tell a story. The Lord had led his family to adopt a little orphan from another country. It was a very moving testimony and it appeared to make everyone listening cry. As he shared about the miracle of adoption and how their hearts were filled with love for this little baby the moment they saw her, it awakened something within me. A scripture I had always loved seemed to explode in significance.

> *"But when the right time came, God sent his Son, born of a woman, subject to the law. God sent him to buy freedom for us who were slaves to the law, so that he could adopt us as his very own children. And because we are his children, God has sent the Spirit of his Son into our hearts, prompting us to call out, 'Abba, Father.' Now you are no longer a slave but God's own child. And since you are his child, God has made you his heir."*
>
> *Galatians 4:4-7 NLT*

Our hyper-individualistic culture in the West typically causes us to emphasize the aspects of our faith that we believe we played a role in. We often speak of accepting Christ as our Savior because *we* like the idea that *we* chose to follow Him. He was asking us to let Him into our lives and *we* decided to open the door. If we experience a sudden shift or breakthrough, we love to reference our prayers as the catalyst. *We* prayed, and *we* believed, and because *we* prayed and *we* believed, God did this wonderful thing. If our finances are going well, and anyone asks, *we* pay our tithes and *we* trust the Lord. We are often far less enthusiastic about aspects of the Kingdom of God that have very little to do with us. This is strange because these non-human aspects reveal the true wonder of God's love for us. Our salvation being an adoption is one of the very best.

In an adoption the child brings nothing to the equation except *need*. Adoption is necessary because they lack anyone to care for them and have no family to belong to. Adoption is based in the love of a father who sees this child as helpless and makes the decision to enlarge his own family by welcoming in a stranger. In adoption, the real testimony is the father and not the adopted child. The child is powerless to change the circumstances and only has a hope and a future because the father, who saw them, decided to love them and take them home. As that child grows up in this new home and benefits from having a family and a new name, the proper response is gratitude and humility. The father is not discouraged by any of the struggles or challenges because he knew all of that was part of choosing the child. In fact, if the adopted child experiences any significant hurt, it is always the other children who cause it by lashing out. The father is the one who offers healing and compassion while reminding the other kids to get along. This is a very practical understanding of our journey with Jesus.

When the good news about Christ penetrated our hearts, our loving Father looked with compassion on unwanted children and extended an invitation to come home with Him.

When we accept, we find ourselves at home in His house. Because we are adopted, He allows us to use His name. Because we are adopted, we have a seat at the family table. We can now spend the rest of our lives learning about this wonderful Father Who wanted us. We end up realizing that He is a pretty big deal by all measures of accounting. There is no limit to what can be accomplished in our lives because of Who He is. The life-changing decision was not one we made. The life-changing decision was His decision to love and accept us!

"Can we boast, then, that we have done anything to be accepted by God? No, because our acquittal is not based on obeying the law. It is based on faith."

Romans 3:27 NLT

Jesus is the One Who makes any of this possible. Not a single aspect of this new life can be credited to us or our religious efforts. It is all Him. Our faith positions us to receive this life but the power of it is entirely of God. When we try to posture ourselves and take credit for our faith, we need to be careful because even that is a gift of God.

"Because of the privilege and authority God has given me, I give each of you this warning: Don't think you are better than you really are. Be honest in your evaluation of yourselves, measuring yourselves by the faith God has given us."

Romans 12:3 NLT

When He reaches out to us and offers us a place in His home, He even helps us believe it so we can receive it. When

THE FAMILY

we are honest with ourselves, as Paul directs us to be, we often remember this. We heard the Gospel once, and then again. Most of us heard it several times. The message came to us in different ways. My mom told me. When she did get us to attend her little church, the minister there would tell it again. My friend and his youth leaders told me a few times. The night I surrendered to Christ, the young evangelist had preached the same Gospel message as all these others. If it was simply a matter of trusting who was talking, I would have responded to all of those before that had shared the message with me. This time it was a stranger. Yet in that moment, faith came into my heart. If I take credit and conclude it was just me deciding to accept Jesus, then that leaves me in control of everything that follows. When I'm more reflective and honest, the amazing grace we sing so often about came to life inside of me. It was God! He came to me in that place and He touched my heart so I could really hear what was being offered to me. He opened my eyes to see it and His love invaded my darkness and helped me not fear coming home. All I said was "Yes"!

> *"He came to his own people, and even they rejected him. But to all who believed him and accepted him, he gave the right to become children of God. They are reborn—not with a physical birth resulting from human passion or plan, but a birth that comes from God."*
>
> John 1:11-13 NLT

Did you see it there? Evangelicals often quote this wonderful passage and emphasize *receiving Jesus*. That possibility only exists because first, He came to His people. When they rejected Him, the implication is He then came to more people. The origin of this new life is Him. Salvation is of the Lord. When we take the time to read through the New Testament, we find this perspective everywhere. Believers were consistently giving Jesus all the glory. We do not use the word glory often today so another word might be *the credit*. Their witness was *look what Jesus has done* and not *look at us and how well we responded to Jesus*.

"Now to Him who is able to do exceedingly abundantly above all that we ask or think, according to the power that works in us, to Him be glory in the church by Jesus Christ to all generations, forever and ever. Amen."

Ephesians 3:20-21 NKJV

Have you ever considered how much more Jesus began to do in your life than you realized when you asked Him into your heart? From the first moment of this new life, He is doing more than we understand. He is doing more than we know to ask for. He is doing more than we *believe*. Every change within us that happens, is only because of His power working in us. Every victory is His. Redemption and every moment of restoration is all sourced back to Jesus living inside of us. This concept of our adoption into His family was virtually unknown to us when we had that inner sense that we needed Jesus. That inner sense came from Him.

THE FAMILY

Jesus was reaching toward us and patiently coaxed us out of the darkness until we ran into His arms. He wanted us in His family.

The months of studying and searching for this perspective on my own salvation did a lot to restore my joy in Christ. I hope that as you meditate on it, joy will rise within you as well. While I was spending my time with Jesus and worshiping Him for choosing me, a song was born in my heart. At first it was a simple chorus that I sang.

> "I am wanted
> I am chosen
> For Your home, by Your hand
> I am forgiven
> I am anointed
> By Your grace, I can stand
> Forever I am Yours
> You're my Father
> You're the Lord"

The more I worshiped Him for this wonderful truth, the more His joy and love filled my life. I had always been grateful that when I called on the Lord, He saved me. Gratitude for His forgiveness and mercy had been the fuel for my praise through all the years I had known Christ. Worship team companions often observed that in almost every song set or list, I sing something about the cross. Jesus paying the price for all of us has always stirred my heart to give Him thanks. That sacrifice is true no matter how my day or week is going. We can always look there and find a reason to sing. This revelation was adding more fuel to my fire. The realization that I know Him only because He reached out to me first, guiding me back home and offering forgiveness, is what fills my heart with song even now.

THE FAMILY

CHAPTER FIVE REFLECTION QUESTIONS

"Welcome to the family table."

1. What does the idea of adopting an orphan child stir within your heart?
2. How do you feel when you consider that the invitation to believe in Jesus was also the Father's invitation to come home to His house?
3. When you think back to the moment of your salvation, how would you describe what God had done to get you to that moment?
4. How does the reality that God chose you to be a part of His family impact your memory of the beginning of your faith journey?
5. How are you inspired by the understanding that your personal level of faith does not limit what the Father is doing in your life?
6. In what ways is your witness to the world potentially impacted by inviting people to *find* a home with God now rather than merely *going to Heaven* later?

"There is enough in God to furnish us with matter of joy in the worst circumstance on earth. Rejoice in the Lord always, and again I say, Rejoice. If good men have not a continual feast, it is their own fault."

—Matthew Henry

CHAPTER SIX

FAMILY MATTERS

"For I am poor and needy, and my heart is wounded within me."

Psalms 109:22 NKJV

The human capacity to hurt and damage our fellow travelers is quite remarkable. Our words have the power to severely wound other people. Our actions, or inactions, can leave a trail of battered hearts and lives behind us. Our decisions regarding investment of our time can leave others wounded with abandonment. Our anger, above all else, can fuel us to do extensive harm to people around us, including the ones we declare we love. The longer we walk our path, the more often we will be involved in interactions with others that leave us wounded. Even with the beautiful organism of the family of God, there are often offenses.

In the verse above, David announces two distinct problems. First was physical lack in that moment of his life. In addition, he recognized a wounded heart within himself. I have experienced both and I would imagine you have as well. Which one is more challenging? When I think back over my life and people I've known along the way, the answer comes into view quickly. There have been folks with very little physical wealth and wounded hearts. There have been others with very little wealth but a whole and healthy heart. The healthy heart prevails, and I have watched them walk with joy and peace that was unshaken by their lack. There have been folks abundantly loaded with wealth and possessions. The wounded heart is so powerful that it will spoil all the fortune and leave a wealthy person miserable and wanting. I think that proves which problem is more severe. A healthy heart brings joy to people, regardless of their physical circumstances. Conversely, a wounded heart can spoil even the most abundant season of life. The Bible, not surprisingly, teaches this.

"Guard your heart above all else, for it determines the course of your life."

Proverbs 4:23 NLT

One version of the Bible refers to the heart within us as *the spring* that feeds our lives. That implication is powerful because it confronts the modern narrative that our environment determines how life unfolds for us. Life is not what is happening to us but rather what flows out of our hearts. Like any settlement on any section of land, the quality of that spring determines the life and health of what is watered by it. A wounded heart, burdened with offense and a desire for vengeance, is like poison in the water. Bitterness is a quality of the soul anchored in unforgiveness for past violations. The choice to hold on to past wounds actually hurts us more than the original offense did. We will only guard our hearts with diligence if we begin to recognize that the condition of our heart is determining the quality of our life.

One of the most detrimental conditions to a life full of the joy of Jesus is carrying wounds and offenses from the past.

Learning to forgive others is like pulling rocks and stones off the outlet of a living well within us. Love, peace, and joy naturally begin to flow in fullness because the Spirit of Christ dwells within us. As we explore reclaiming our joy, we need to carefully consider the journey we have made and how many wounds our heart received along the way. This is not an exercise in endlessly rehearsing what has happened for the purpose of assigning blame and shifting responsibility. This is the recognition that other humans can harm us deeply, and all of those wounds will affect the health of our hearts. We will always find that the joy of the Lord is not easily retained in a heart full of wounds. If you think back, are there certain individuals, during certain interactions, that have wounded your heart? The honest answer is a resounding yes. Have you received the healing ministry of the Spirit to forgive those offenders and leave that pain behind? The honest answer to this is usually far more complicated.

"An offended friend is harder to win back than a fortified city. Arguments separate friends like a gate locked with bars."

Proverbs 18:19 NLT

We have all experienced the *wall building* and *gate closing* that is our natural response to wounds and offenses. It can happen within us almost subconsciously. The wound occurs and we build a defensive position between the offender and our own soul. It is the same instinct for self-preservation that causes us to pull away from a hot stove or remember the burn it caused forever. If your words or actions are wounding my heart, then I will quickly construct a barrier between us so that your choices are no longer wounding me. In the heat of the moment it is natural, and there is actually very little direct teaching in the Scripture to suggest that the initial response is anything to worry about. It is the decision we make after the wound that has the power to cripple us.

When the shock of a wound or offense dissipates, we are left with the facts of what happened. This becomes the more important moment because what happens next is up to us. The original wound can occur when we have little or even no control over what happened. It almost always surprises us when someone we trust betrays us, or people we love turn and hurt us. So often the initial encounter and damage was orchestrated by another person. When it is over, we are back in control and our decision is extremely important. Are we going to carry it with us, or are we going to forgive it and move on?

Recently, I watched an interesting conversation on a talk show between two famous women. Both of them have walked through fairly well-reported divorces in recent years. As they chatted about their pain and their lives after the fact, it was abundantly clear which one had moved on to wholeness, and which had not. I would imagine every person watching was able to make the distinction. We could all hear it in the words spoken and the sentiments shared. At one point, the recovered one shared a powerful piece of wisdom. "As soon as you realize that you have a choice in what you do with the pain, everything can change." On a foundational level, this is true for all humans. On a spiritual level, this is potentially transformational for the believer. The Spirit of Christ dwells within us.

If you are reading this and recognizing you have a wounded heart, please keep reading. Sometimes the pain and the narrative we have written around it will make us recoil and retreat at the thought of simply forgiving our adversary. A flood of strong feelings can result from just thinking about that person. We must carefully consider what scripture teaches us about this.

"Get rid of all bitterness, rage, anger, harsh words, and slander, as well as all types of evil behavior. Instead, be kind to each other, tenderhearted, forgiving one another, just as God through Christ has forgiven you."

Ephesians 4:31-32 NLT

With regularity, we read a passage like this and see it from a place of religious performance. In order to be a good Christian we need to be nice. In reality, most of the scripture is written from a place of sincere love for the Church and desire to see all believers whole and restored. We reflect Jesus to this fallen world. It is for our own good and well-being to get rid of all bitterness. We are restored within when we choose to forgive one another. These words are given to the Church, so there is no surprise that we retain the ability to wound one another after we meet Jesus. As a follower of Jesus, one of the most liberating facts revealed here is that we get to *choose*.

Our culture is bombarding us with a huge lie in this present moment. It is the deception that our feelings are actually facts. How we feel is being held up as the standard against which all other information is judged. Truth is only truth if I feel like I can embrace it and it benefits me. If I feel like your statement makes me uncomfortable, I can simply reject it because of how it makes me feel. The extension of this reasoning is that the other person is *making me feel* like this. I can then only forgive them if I can manage to stop feeling hurt with them. Since I have no control over my feelings, I am left in bondage to what they did to me.

While professional counseling can be a powerful tool for healing, it's important to recognize that true growth comes when we take responsibility for our own responses, rather than solely blaming others for how we feel. The risk is that if we place all the focus on our feelings, we may end up constantly evaluating our progress based on emotional comfort rather than truth. When we let our emotions dictate our actions and define the value of others, we fall into a cycle of relying on temporary relief. In this mindset, feelings drive every decision, reaction, and perception of others. But relying solely on emotions as our guide can be misleading; truth is not determined by how we feel.

FAMILY MATTERS

The only way for a Christian to follow Christ into maturity is establishing proper order within themselves.

Jesus is the foundation and His truth is the standard. The facts are what our Creator teaches us. All of our feelings and emotions, no matter how strong, are temporary expressions of our flesh and can be controlled, even transformed, by the truth and the power of the Spirit of Truth within us. This entire conversation is about recovering our joy rather than simply allowing ourselves to walk without it. If I can walk toward my joy, I can also walk away from my bitterness. If I can move deliberately toward fullness of life, I can also immediately move away from rage and anger. The same power I had to choose the pursuit of my joy, is the power I have to choose to forgive others and be whole. Our spiritual adversary loves to convince us that we are somehow stuck with how we feel when nothing could be further from the truth.

If you read this wounded, you may be thinking, "How could I possibly just forgive them?" I have been wounded numerous times and I can tell you that the words of Paul work. They are not always easy to walk out, but the pathway is clear. Look at the verse again and find the source of mercy.

"Instead, be kind to each other, tenderhearted, forgiving one another, just as God through Christ has forgiven you."

Ephesians 4:32 NLT

An amazing revelation is sitting in front of our eyes. How did God, in His perfect holiness, find His way to forgiving me? The answer is declared here. *Through Christ*, He forgave me. *Through Christ* He forgave you. When we consider the words, we are turned toward a confrontation with our culture again. The modern answer would be that God is able to forgive us all because of how much He *feels* love for us. Biblically, that logic does not hold up for very long. God does not forgive because of His feelings. God forgives because Jesus paid the price for all the sin that covers us. Forgiveness flows toward us because all of the judgment was placed upon Him. The sin is very real and God is not pretending it didn't happen and looking the other way out of kindness. The sin is cancelled because of the sacrifice that pays the debt created by the failure.

Most often, the barrier within us to forgiving another person is the perception we carry that they need to *pay* for what they did. We may not say it out loud, but inside of our hearts the scales are out of balance and an injustice has occurred. Can you remember those old balance scales? Two little pans hanging from a balanced arm above. Our emotions work that way. We pile all of our pain on one side and it pushes it down to the bottom. Then we sit waiting for the person who hurt us to do something to balance our scale. We may feel the scales are balanced by their apology. We may feel the scales are balanced by their suffering. We may feel they can never do anything that could balance the scales because the pain *feels* too great. We cannot survive if we lose sight of Jesus and His sacrifice. Forgiveness flows through Christ. Jesus paid the price for all of my sin. Jesus also paid the price for all of their sin, which includes their sin against me. Our heart demands that they pay for what they did and Heaven's response is that Someone else already paid for it!

Jesus hanging in agony on the cross was praying for the forgiveness of the people who were killing Him. How was that possible? What possible reason could the Father have to forgive the fallen and sinful people who were murdering His innocent Son? The only answer given to us is that His sacrifice, even in that moment, was providing enough atonement to cover their sin.

"But he was pierced for our rebellion, crushed for our sins. He was beaten so we could be whole. He was whipped so we could be healed. All of us, like sheep, have strayed away. We have left God's paths to follow our own. Yet the Lord laid on him the sins of us all."

Isaiah 53:5-6 NLT

We can forgive if we recognize that the person who has wounded us is simply a fallen human just like us. We have fallen just as short of perfection in our lives as they have in theirs. Even if we have not committed their specific sin against another person, we have committed many others, against many others. Jesus paid the price for all of this. The same mercy we embrace can be extended to someone else.

> **The same joy we found when God canceled our debt, we can receive again as we forgive their debt to us.**

When our fallen carnal nature calls out for judgment on the offender, we turn our fallen heart toward the cross of Jesus Christ. It is there that the judgment we deserved was placed upon Someone else. Any judgment that we think they deserve was also placed upon Christ in that precious moment of redemptive sacrifice.

One day the disciples were walking along with Jesus and the topic of offense and forgiveness came up. Peter came to Jesus and asked, "Lord, how often should I forgive someone who sins against me? Seven times?" For some reason, I always picture Jesus pausing and smiling at a moment like this. He knows Peter is trying and He knows that the others are listening. In His answer, He gives Peter all the power. "No, not seven times, but seventy times seven!" (Mathew 18:21-22) The answer to that math equation is 490 times! I cannot speak for you, but the worst people in my life have never come close to sinning against me 490 times. It seems obvious that Jesus was not teaching a formula in which we keep score and call for judgment on sin number 491. He was teaching the principle that our forgiveness must vastly exceed what seems religiously or practically possible. He also made no reference to how anyone was going to feel about it. In the parable that followed, He contrasted the abundance of God's mercy and forgiveness with our willingness to withhold mercy and forgiveness. The end of the parable is quite strongly worded.

"Then the king called in the man he had forgiven and said, 'You evil servant! I forgave you that tremendous debt because you pleaded with me. Shouldn't you have mercy on your fellow servant, just as I had mercy on you?'"

Matthew 18:32-33 NLT

This is one of the harshest rebukes Jesus gave. If we find ourselves in need of correction in this area, then let us receive it and repent. Also consider that a wonderful opportunity is available to us, just as it was to the man in this parable. He had received the forgiveness of a lifetime of debt that he could not possibly pay. He had gone on his way free of that debt by the declaration of the King! He then had the power to extend that same mercy and forgiveness to his fellow servant for a much smaller debt. He had the power to set them free and give them their joy as well. If he had chosen forgiveness, everyone involved walks away free. It was his choice to make when considering what he believed the other man owed him. In the light of the King and his mercy, the choice should have been very easy to make.

When we are faced with this decision, our choice should be just as clear and easy to make. Extend mercy and forgive as we have been forgiven.

Every truly joyful believer I have ever known has possessed a forgiving spirit. They look at other people *through Christ* and simply let things go. They are so thankful for the mercy they have been given that they find no room in their hearts to hold others accountable for their sins and failings. Releasing all the judgment and accountability to God, they walk away free. I have found the same freedom and it is wonderful. Every time the actions of another person somehow wound my heart, I am faced again with the same decision. Each time I hold their sin and my pain inside, I can feel my own joy in Christ begin to suffocate. Like a starving fire that is burning low and turning into ash, my own joy vanishes away. Each time I turn toward the cross and see the sacrifice of Jesus for all of my sin and all of theirs as well, I find the mercy I need, and the mercy to offer them. Nothing seems more like Jesus than forgiving another person. Nothing restores my own soul faster than setting the captives free.

The writer of the book of Hebrews spoke of this necessary forgiveness. He also introduced a wonderful word picture to the whole situation.

"Look after each other so that none of you fails to receive the grace of God. Watch out that no poisonous root of bitterness grows up to trouble you, corrupting many."

Hebrews 12:15 NLT

Bitterness from unforgiveness grows slowly in our hearts like a poisonous weed. That is remarkable to consider. The weeds in our yards give us a hint about the wisdom the writer is sharing with the Church. I have never planted a single weed. Have you? They seem to just happen. I can spend hours and dollars on my lawn and still have my weeds grow greener and faster than my grass. If I ignore them for very long, they can become quite thick and strong. They also begin to kill everything growing around them because they use all the nutrients and moisture in the soil. When I decide to get rid of these nasty things, I am presented with two options. I can mow off the tops of them and they seem to blend with my lawn making everything look better. The alternative is to get down on my knees and pull them up by the root.

FAMILY MATTERS

The first choice is easier and more immediately satisfying but does not actually get rid of the root of the weed. It is still there and poisoning the ground around it. In appearance, I dealt with it, but upon closer inspection I have not addressed the problem. This is how we deal with offenses and wounds in the modern church with far too great a frequency. We work to hide the injury, the bitterness, and the poison flowing from it. We learn how to look very healed and healthy. We know what to say and how to act. Yet within our hearts, the wound, the offender, and the bitterness remains. We are hiding it from others but it is poisoning our lives anyway.

The decision to pull the weeds up by their roots is far more work. I have to get down close to it. I have to put my hands around the root. Pulling with some force, it comes out of the ground. Removed from the soil, it can be discarded and left to dry in the sun. One at a time—with thorns and all—I can do the hard work of digging up the weeds. This strategy does not produce an instantaneous improvement in appearance. Over the course of time, however, the results are far better. Removing the roots of bitterness is the only mature decision for a believer. The wounds of others plant the seeds of bitterness. As soon as we see it growing up and overshadowing our joy, we must set ourselves to pull it from the roots. We pull it and discard it by forgiving the person we are blaming for the injury. We watch what they did dry up in the light of the Son and blow away in the wind. We remove the poison of it from our hearts and it stops corrupting the growth of the fruit of His Spirit within us. Then our joy returns!

One question remains. If we are skilled at hiding wounds and pretending we are not bitter, how do we recognize it? How do we honestly evaluate whether we carry bitterness in our hearts toward another person? The answer is easier than most people realize. It is so easy that it will sound almost anticlimactic. Have you ever tasted something bitter? One of the first things you notice is that you cannot stop the muscles in your face from reacting to it. The taste triggers a physical response that everyone can see. That is usually the reason others start laughing if they have duped you into tasting something bitter. The face you make is funny. It is also unmistakable. When you think of who hurt you what happens to your face? It may sound like I'm attempting to be humorous about this, but I am not. Emotional bitterness will show up on your face just as tangibly as licking a lime. If someone else brings up the offender in conversation, what happens on your face? Your body language will tell you the story. When you focus on your best friend, beloved children, or grandchildren, a smile comes to your face. When you think about your old adversary, something else happens to your face if you still carry bitterness. If you make a face like you just licked a lime, then you know that you have some weeds to pull!

Look at them through Christ. Recognize that mercy is coming to you from our Father in Heaven, through His Son. Make the choice to release that mercy toward the offender and forgive them from your heart. Ask the Spirit to cleanse your soul from all bitterness and to redeem your memories so that you can move on. Set the captive free by the power of the Spirit in your life just like Christ announced He was going to do. Jesus already paid for the sin they committed against you. His blood was sufficient to cover it completely, just like all of your sins were washed away. Let your joy return by embracing the beauty of a forgiving heart. That is far more like Christ than keeping score and searching for judgment.

FAMILY MATTERS

CHAPTER SIX REFLECTION QUESTIONS

"The family God gave me."

1. How has your understanding of being part of God's family shaped the way you approach relationships with those around you?
2. What lessons have you learned from the challenges of navigating relationships within your earthly family that could apply to your spiritual family?
3. Consider the times when you've felt disconnected or misunderstood within the body of Christ. How did you respond, and what might you do differently now?
4. Ephesians 2:19 reminds us that we are "members of God's household." What does this truth mean for how you invest in your church community?
5. How can embracing the forgiveness and grace you've received from Christ help you to extend those same gifts to your family, both earthly and spiritual?
6. What practical steps can you take to foster unity and love in the family of God, even when conflicts arise?

"Joy is not necessarily the absence of suffering,
it is the presence of God."

—Sam Storms

CHAPTER SEVEN

THE ADVERSARY

One of the most tangible pieces of evidence that you have changed citizenship to the Kingdom of Light is the constant resistance and warfare of the darkness. When we live in the darkness before coming to Christ, it is literally all we have ever known. Our adversary is very content with that arrangement because the darkness is his domain. The more captives he can keep there and keep lying to, the more satisfied he is in his honor fight with God. We live almost completely unaware of this until the light of Jesus shines into our hearts.

"I will say to the prisoners, 'Come out in freedom,' and to those in darkness, 'Come into the light.' They will be my sheep, grazing in green pastures and on hills that were previously bare."

Isaiah 49:9 NLT

"For God, who said, 'Let there be light in the darkness,' has made this light shine in our hearts so we could know the glory of God that is seen in the face of Jesus Christ."

2 Corinthians 4:6 NLT

Remember when we talked about the Kingdom of God? When we choose to follow Jesus and we open our hearts to His stirring invitation to live, we are moved from one kingdom to the other. It is like one of those hostage rescue missions portrayed on movie screens. The captives in the dark are picked up and taken away to another Kingdom.

> *"For he has rescued us from the kingdom of darkness and transferred us into the Kingdom of his dear Son,"*
>
> Colossians 1:13 NLT

Our departure from the darkness is one of the sources of all the changes that seem to follow salvation. We see things differently because we are now in the light. We see ourselves differently and go from living on feelings alone—like people in darkness have to do—to growing in true knowledge and understanding. We see far more clearly around us because light is now revealing the roots and reasons for the behaviors we witness day in and day out. We become far more aware of sin because we see the contrast of that darkness to the white robes of righteousness given to us by Christ. Things that used to be perfectly acceptable to us become unclean and wretched. We can now see God's hand at work in circumstances around us that we used to dismiss as chance or luck. We are now children of light!

> *"But you aren't in the dark about these things, dear brothers and sisters, and you won't be surprised when the day of the Lord comes like a thief. For you are all children of the light and of the day; we don't belong to darkness and night."*
>
> 1 Thessalonians 5:4-5 NLT

THE ADVERSARY

Whenever our adversary, Satan, loses his hold on any of his captives, it infuriates him. His fallen contention is that people prefer sin and darkness and live to dishonor God and ignore His commandments with all their strength. He sees himself as the head rebel amidst all the other rebels. Rebellion against God's authority is the one common theme which permeates his entire kingdom. He chose rebellion over obedience. He chose to rise up in pride rather than to fall down in humility. He chose to take the throne rather than to serve the One Who sat on it. In his rebellion, he failed miserably.

"When the seventy-two disciples returned, they joyfully reported to him, 'Lord, even the demons obey us when we use your name!' 'Yes,' he told them, 'I saw Satan fall from heaven like lightning!'"

Luke 10:17-18 NLT

"How you are fallen from heaven, O shining star, son of the morning! You have been thrown down to the earth, you who destroyed the nations of the world. For you said to yourself, 'I will ascend to heaven and set my throne above God's stars. I will preside on the mountain of the gods far away in the north. I will climb to the highest heavens and be like the Most High.' Instead, you will be brought down to the place of the dead, down to its lowest depths."

Isaiah 14:12-15 NLT

One of the very first scriptural references to this fact is the beginning of Job.

> *"One day the members of the heavenly court came to present themselves before the Lord, and the Accuser, Satan, came with them. 'Where have you come from?' The Lord asked Satan. Satan answered the Lord, 'I have been patrolling the earth, watching everything that's going on.'"*
>
> *Job 1:6-7 NLT*

In the minds of many intellectuals, the idea of there being a real "devil" is just foolishness. They dismiss the notion as nothing more than the leftover ideologies of fables and legends about good and evil. Those who do not follow Jesus are allowed this freedom of deliberate blindness. If they choose to ignore the teachings of Jesus, as well as the millions of testimonies of those who have found spiritual freedom in Christ, the results for them are sadly predictable. They sit in the darkness and do not realize it because darkness is all they have ever known. They continue to function on feelings and instincts. They have only themselves to rely on, and they are spiritually blind. Mix in a little pride and you have a blind person sitting in the darkness telling everyone walking in the light how stupid they are for believing in light!

> *"Gently instruct those who oppose the truth. Perhaps God will change those people's hearts, and they will learn the truth. Then they will come to their senses and escape from the devil's trap. For they have been held captive by him to do whatever he wants."*
>
> *2 Timothy 2:25-26 NLT*

Those of us who have escaped become targets. Think of one of those old movies about the guy who escapes from the prison work camp and is on the run. The old warden does not simply accept it. The escape represents an insult and an implication of weakness. It becomes personal and the warden will do anything, legal or otherwise, to recapture the escapee. All the best movies about this would have the hound dogs running through the forest and looking for the scent. Once they have the trail, their mission is to run down the fugitive. It is the root behind the phrase, "I am going to hound you until you do it." The dogs give the prisoner no time to rest or regroup and make a plan. Eventually, the dogs are almost always able to corner the escapee and take them back to prison. Fortunately for us, the *hounds of hell* cannot run us down because they cannot climb the walls that surround the Kingdom of God. They end up barking at the gates and snarling at the fence.

"So Christ has truly set us free. Now make sure that you stay free, and don't get tied up again in slavery to the law."

Galatians 5:1 NLT

In the Old Testament book of Isaiah, we find a wonderful declaration God made about Jesus and His ministry. Notice these words:

"I, the Lord, have called you to demonstrate my righteousness. I will take you by the hand and guard you, and I will give you to my people, Israel, as a symbol of my covenant with them. And you will be a light to guide the nations. You will open the eyes of the blind. You will free the captives from prison, releasing those who sit in dark dungeons."

Isaiah 42:6-7 NLT

It was another reading from the same book that Jesus used in His first public preaching.

> *"The scroll of Isaiah the prophet was handed to him. He unrolled the scroll and found the place where this was written: 'The Spirit of the Lord is upon me, for he has anointed me to bring Good News to the poor. He has sent me to proclaim that captives will be released, that the blind will see, that the oppressed will be set free, and that the time of Lord's favor has come.' He rolled up the scroll, handed it back to the attendant, and sat down. All the eyes in the synagogue looked at him intently. Then he began to speak to them. "This Scripture you've just heard has been fulfilled this very day!"*
>
> Luke 4:17-21 NLT

The believer is free in Christ! Many need clarification at this point because we need to understand the concept of freedom. Freedom is mine, which means the choices are mine. Our Father's goal in setting us free was not to create holy robots that were programmed to always do what was right. His goal was restoration of our freedom and our sight so that we could choose, from a heart of love, to do what is right. Instead of being blind and following feelings and instincts, we are alive and seeing clearly what our actions mean and who is whispering to us in the background. We see clearly the goodness and love of God. Just as clearly, we see the depravity and destruction of the sinful nature. The enemy can no longer control us. Our chains are lying at our feet and we are captives no more. The Father does not control us because that was never what He wanted. We are free.

THE ADVERSARY

We stand in the Kingdom of God fully capable of living lives that honor our King, and fully aware that our King is worthy of such a life.

I have never seen a video of someone walking out of jail who did not look happy. Joy is the natural reaction to freedom. When our perspective is renewed by the truth, we are able to walk in that joy even when we make a wrong choice. Think about it. *We* made the wrong choice. Nobody was able to make the choice for us! We can learn from it, grow in our understanding, and receive the grace and mercy of God. We can apply wisdom, walk in repentance, and never make that choice again. Why? Because we are *free*. That freedom brings great responsibility. We must learn the ways of God. As His Word illuminates our path, we become more skilled at avoiding snares and traps. We become more efficient at recognizing the lies and deceptions of our adversary. His influence is reduced to just his voice now, though he loves to talk. Our continued victory requires some vigilance.

"Stay alert! Watch out for your great enemy, the devil. He prowls around like a roaring lion, looking for someone to devour. Stand firm against him, and be strong in your faith. Remember that your family of believers all over the world is going through the same kind of suffering you are."

1 Peter 5:8-9 NLT

The battle is real. But our focus is not on the details of spiritual warfare. That is an entire topic worthy of study all on its own. Paul speaks of the battle. Peter gives instructions about it. James gives us some strategy. On the island Patmos, the Apostle John received the revelation, and with it, many amazing images of the reality of the spiritual world and war around us. Our emphasis is on the broader scene of this entire situation. We will take more of a high altitude look. The conflict between the two kingdoms is varied and multidimensional. The battle itself speaks to a wider truth that can fuel our joy. You may already be thinking, "How can our spiritual battle inspire joy?" It is all a matter of perspective. Consider the opening of Jude's letter to the church.

"This letter is from Jude, a slave of Jesus Christ and a brother of James. I am writing to all who have been called by God the Father, who loves you and keeps you safe in the care of Jesus Christ."

Jude 1 NLT

A few paragraphs later and this brother declares the same truth a slightly different way.

"Now all glory to God, who is able to keep you from falling away and will bring you with great joy into his glorious presence without a single fault."

Jude 24 NLT

The battle is real, but that reality also speaks to the truth. You have an adversary if you are a follower of Jesus. He hates you and the freedom Christ has given you. He breathes out threats and lies and seeks to inspire people around you to hurt and deceive you. He would love nothing more than to dishonor Jesus by snatching you away and causing you to fall. Yet here you are. You are reading this book. Your faith—while most certainly not perfect—is intact. Your desire to follow Jesus remains. You have some scars, but you are standing. You have had disappointments, but you are not turning back. Jude causes us to know that our continued survival is a testimony to God's keeping power! We often sing about holding on to Jesus, but the more powerful reality is that Jesus is holding on to us.

> *"My sheep listen to my voice; I know them, and they follow me. I give them eternal life, and they will never perish. No one can snatch them away from me, for my Father has given them to me, and he is more powerful than anyone else. No one can snatch them from the Father's hand."*
>
> John 10:27-29 NLT

Every single day that your faith endures is a testimony to the goodness of God! You are not still in this race because of your commitment to Jesus. You are not still standing because of your faith and all the scripture you have memorized. You are not still looking for the promises of God because of all the worship songs you love. You are still standing because Jesus lives inside of you and He has not let you fall. Peter warned us about our adversary. He called him the roving devourer.

Every day that you are not devoured is a testimony to the faithfulness of God.

Jesus told us that Satan was the father of lies. Each day that you have sifted through the lies and made your stand upon the truth is a witness to the strength of God's hold on you. Every trial you survive is a praise to God. Every temptation you sidestepped is a praise to God. Every time you got back up after you entertained a temptation is a praise to God. Every time another person's wounds caused you pain and you still rose in the morning and followed Christ is a praise to God. You are standing because Jesus is standing inside of you. The battle is proof that we really are children of God. Our survival is proof that Jesus is the King and He is holding us. All of that releases *joy* in our hearts.

> *"All praise to God, the Father of our Lord Jesus Christ. It is by his great mercy that we have been born again, because God raised Jesus Christ from the dead. Now we live with great expectation, and we have a priceless inheritance—an inheritance that is kept in heaven for you, pure and undefiled, beyond the reach of change and decay. And through your faith, God is protecting you by his power until you receive this salvation, which is ready to be revealed on the last day for all to see. So be truly glad. There is a wonderful joy ahead, even though you must endure many trials for a little while. These trials will show that your faith is genuine. It is being tested as fire tests and purifies gold—though your faith is far more precious than mere gold. So when your faith remains strong through many trials, it will bring you much praise and glory and honor on the day when Jesus Christ is revealed to the whole world."*
>
> 1 Peter 1:3-7 NLT

Every time we survive the fight and endure the testing, we prove our faith is genuine and our God is greater! All of that should help us realize what an amazing gift our faith is and how incredibly faithful Jesus is to those who trust Him. If you look back and see a series of struggles and battles that you have overcome, allow that to fuel your joy. Jesus is real and you really belong to Him. That is why you have not been overcome.

CHAPTER SEVEN REFLECTION QUESTIONS

"From darkness to light should be easier."

1. If you put on a blindfold and lived in your house for a day without your sight, how would you navigate? What would that teach you about life before Christ?
2. Every writer of scripture speaks of the reality of our adversary, the Devil. Why do you think so many in modern times attempt to dismiss his existence?
3. How does the imagery of a rescue mission bringing you to safety in another kingdom affect your understanding of spiritual warfare and adversity?
4. In what way(s) do you think believers misunderstand the declaration that they are *free* in Christ?
5. How can our spiritual battles be used to inspire our joy in Christ?

———

"Never let anything so fill you with sorrow as to make you forget the joy of the Christ risen."

—Saint Mother Teresa of Calcutta

CHAPTER EIGHT

THE SACRIFICE

When we speak of the adversary and the victory of Jesus, we cannot shift our focus from Calvary. On the cross, Jesus won the victory. Some modern congregations act as if this is too old-fashioned to remain part of our modern narrative. I submit to you that if we take the cross of Christ away, we have no narrative at all. It is on the cross that the pure blood of our Savior was shed and all of those who are guilty could be forgiven. It was there that the price for our freedom was paid and redemption became possible. Hanging on that cursed tree, Jesus broke the power of the curse for all of us!

> *"You were dead because of your sins and because your sinful nature was not yet cut away. Then God made you alive with Christ, for he forgave all our sins. He canceled the record of the charges against us and took it away by nailing it to the cross. In this way, he disarmed the spiritual rulers and authorities. He shamed them publicly by his victory over them on the cross."*
>
> *Colossians 2:13-15 NLT*

AMAZED AGAIN

Our forgiveness flows from the cross. Throughout the history of the Church, every generation has understood this. We find it reflected over and over in the music written for the worship of Christian congregations.

> *Jesus paid it all*
> *All to Him I owe*
> *Sin had left a crimson stain*
> *He washed it white as snow*

> *At the cross, at the cross*
> *Where I first saw the light*
> *And the burden of my heart rolled away*
> *It was there by faith*
> *I received my sight*
> *And now I am happy all the day*

> *There Your mercy and Your grace was free*
> *There Your pardon multiplied to me*
> *There my burdened soul found liberty*
> *At Calvary*

The great Apostle Paul wrote of the power of the cross in nearly every epistle that he authored. The references could fill an entire book of their own. I love the crescendo he builds to at the end of the letter to Galatia.

"As for me, may I never boast about anything except the cross of our Lord Jesus Christ."

Galatians 6:14 NLT

THE SACRIFICE

One of the main reasons that the cross and the sacrifice made there should inspire joy within our hearts is because it reminds us all of our value to God. People wonder if God truly loves us. It was proven at the cross. People wonder if sin is a real problem or merely a religious concept. Then we see Jesus dying to cover those sins at the cross. People argue about Jesus being the only way for men to be saved. Then we search history and find no other great leader dying to pay the price for our sins. Jesus alone took our place and paid that awful price. Where the vast majority of religious leaders demand the people who follow them make all the sacrifices, Jesus stands before us and makes the supreme sacrifice Himself. In doing that, He proves His love. His love should bring us joy. He offers forgiveness of sin. Forgiveness should bring us joy. He displays the mercy of God as the innocent pays the price for the guilty. Mercy should bring us joy. Looking at the cross should make the believer rejoice!

Paul appears to anchor our entire *living sacrifice* of service and devotion to Jesus and the cross when writing to the Roman church.

"And so, dear brothers and sisters, I plead with you to give your bodies to God because of all he has done for you. Let them be a living and holy sacrifice—the kind he will find acceptable. This is truly the way to worship him."

Romans 12:1 NLT

He is teaching that our Christian life is actually our response to what God has already done. (That is powerful in an age when so many try to teach various aspects of faith and obedience as the catalysts to getting God to do something for us.) We are responding to Him. He initiated all of this, which is why He is called the *Author* of our faith in Hebrews. Where did He do this? He has displayed His goodness and love for us in every aspect of our existence, but nowhere more vividly than the cross.

"But God showed his great love for us by sending Christ to die for us while we were still sinners."

Romans 5:8 NLT

When we look at Jesus surrendering His life on the tree for us, our response becomes surrendering our lives in the service of His Kingdom. If we are aware of His sacrifice, then our lives—even when difficult—seem reasonable. I can give my hands in service to the One Who had His hands nailed to the cross. When we see His feet pierced, it makes perfect sense to use our feet to spread that good news. If Jesus can pray from the cross and forgive the people killing Him, then I can certainly forgive those who trespass against *me*. His sacrifice provides a great amount of clarity to my journey. When the will of God is painful and difficult, Jesus obviously understands this. When the people we try to serve turn and spit in our faces, He understands this too. Keep your eyes on Jesus. He is the price God was willing to pay to redeem us.

"For you know that God paid a ransom to save you from the empty life you inherited from your ancestors. And it was not paid with mere gold or silver, which lose their value. It was the precious blood of Christ, the sinless, spotless Lamb of God. God

THE SACRIFICE

chose him as your ransom long before the world began, but now in these last days he has been revealed for your sake."

1 Peter 1:18-20 NLT

Like many things, our appreciation for the cross and His sacrifice can fade. We started off considering how, as humans, fallible and sinful, our joy fades. In this area it is no different, and that is a tragedy. The "spirit of religion" is considered by many the most blinding of all deceptive ideologies. In religion, you can carefully practice rituals about wonderful truths until the truths the ritual celebrates are no longer wonderful. Throughout the Old Testament we see God calling to His people and trying to shake them out of ritual and back into living faith. This weakness in us is only slightly improved as Jesus initiates the transition of the Testaments. He passes the cup during the last supper and announces a 'New Covenant' in His blood. He then instructs His followers to take the meal often and remember. It would seem impossible for us to forget. Our Savior died for us and created a new way. History reveals that He was right to challenge us to remember because we often seem to forget. Christians are able to lose sight of love, mercy, kindness, and grace, even with a communion cup in our hands.

Does the sacrifice Jesus made for you still stir your heart? Has the steady flow of reminders about the cross of Christ eroded your awe and gratitude? Have you partaken in communion until the elements have lost their meaning? If this happens to us, we lose many valuable things and one of them is our joy. The joy that should live in our hearts when we see the price our Savior paid for us will fade if we allow our vision of the cross to be obscured by religious practice and routine. We have to stop often and look to that mountaintop if we are to retain a right perspective. Kneel again in the dirt at the base of the cross and look up. See Jesus there, struggling to breathe and bleeding everywhere to purchase a new life for you.

This quest to rediscover my joy also caused another song to be born in my heart.

In the weeks and months that followed the pandemic, working at a local church had turned into nothing but work. It all felt like labor, and a lot of the love seemed distant. People were gone and spirits were low. My times of prayer had again turned very personal. Searching for my joy in the Lord, this prayer rose in my spirit:

> *Help me see the beauty of Your blood upon the tree*
> *Awaken my wonder at the mercy You've shown me*
> *Restore my soul so my heart can comprehend*
> *What Your amazing grace has done for me again*
> *When I see, I will sing*
> *Of Your love, and Your offering*
> *You are holy, You are worthy*
> *Of all the glory, and all the praise*
> *You are holy, You are worthy*
> *Of all the glory, and all the praise*

THE SACRIFICE

For months I would be alone, often with my keyboard, and sing this prayer. Lord *help!* When it was new and fresh, it all inspired me. Now His sacrifice felt academic and that was an insult to Christ. Thankfully, He answers prayer. A familiar love for the sacrifice Jesus made rose higher and higher in my heart. I began to *see* it again. I began to feel love in response to it again. Joy was being restored and it gave me great strength. Because we quite naturally talk to others about things that bring us joy, my witness was improved. I found myself re-engaging with people when I crossed their paths and telling them how good Jesus was. Any doubt I encountered in them was an opportunity to remind them that Jesus died for us all. Nobody we have ever known loves us more than that.

Consider with me a few statements found in Psalms 111.

"How amazing are the deeds of the Lord! All who delight in him should ponder them." verse 2

"He causes us to remember his wonderful works. How gracious and merciful is our Lord!" verse 4

"He has paid a full ransom for his people. He has guaranteed his covenant with them forever. What a holy, awe-inspiring name he has!" verse 9

"Praise Him forever!" verse 10b

Whenever we feel the dull blanket of religion and ritual settling over the fire in our hearts, we must seek the Lord. The ritual itself may not be bad, but if our hearts are growing cold, that is never good. Jesus is worthy of His people *loving*

Him and rejoicing in what He has done. He will help us remember what moved us before if we will recognize it is gone and call on His Name. Instead of excusing our lack of joy as Christian maturity, we must see it as familiarity and rise above it. At the cross, we see a loving Savior paying an incredible price that proves He loves us! That alone should inspire rejoicing. When we remember all the other wonderful things that flow out from His sacrifice, we should find ourselves shouting. Because Jesus paid the price, we can be forgiven. Forgiven, we are able to come into relationship with Him. Living inside of us, Jesus begins to transform everything. Adopted into His family, we now have a home and place. That place is inside the Kingdom of God, which is eternal and will never be shaken. This wonderous gift of life has also set us free from the darkness and taken us beyond the reach of our adversary. We seem to be collecting many reasons to have joy!

"Always be full of joy in the Lord. I say it again—rejoice!"

Philippians 4:4 NLT

"But let all who take refuge in you rejoice; let them sing joyful praises forever. Spread your protection over them, that all who love your name may be filled with joy."

Psalms 5:11 NLT

CHAPTER EIGHT REFLECTION QUESTIONS

"The Old Rugged Cross."

1. Can you remember and write down the lyrics to a worship song or hymn that celebrates the cross of Christ?

2. In the area of sacrifice, what is the primary difference between Jesus and all of the other "famous" religious leaders of history?

3. How does the idea of our Christian lives being our response to what Jesus has done on the cross affect your view of the walk of faith?

4. When you think back to the last time you participated in a communion service, do you remember it stirring your joy and love for Jesus?

5. What explanations and excuses do you find you make for lacking joy in serving Jesus? In light of His sacrifice upon the cross, how do you begin to feel about those excuses?

"We need to discover all over again that worship is natural to the Christian, as it was to the godly Israelites who wrote the psalms, and that the habit of celebrating the greatness and graciousness of God yields an endless flow of thankfulness, joy, and zeal."

—J.I. Packer

CHAPTER NINE

THE SPIRIT

Christ living inside of us is the source of everything eternal and good. His influence, by His Spirit, brings light and restoration to our darkened hearts. Because of this new light, we can see. His light within us reveals truth to us so that we can understand the ways of His Kingdom. Light exposes deeds formerly hidden in that darkness, and so we become aware of sin. His presence within us causes a new character to grow. It happens quite naturally if we have truly been born again. Paul describes it as *fruit*.

"But the Holy Spirit produces this kind of fruit in our lives: love, joy, peace, patience, kindness, goodness, faithfulness, gentleness, and self-control. There is no law against these things!"

Galatians 5:22-23 NLT

A great many Christians incorrectly read this as a to-do list. With great effort, they set about acting loving, peaceful, and kind. Far too many of us have endured the painful interaction of someone pretending to be loving. Everyone knows it is not quite sincere, and the time slows to a crawl until it is over. These character traits are not assignments. They are described as *fruit*. When you observe any fruit tree with branches sagging with a ripe harvest, you are not looking at anyone's effort or labor. Fruit trees grow fruit. The fruit just happens if their roots are in good soil and there is adequate moisture. In addition, the fruit identifies the tree. With no collegiate training in botany, we can pull an apple from a tree and know with certainty that it is an apple tree. It is very simple in application. Paul is describing the same simple inner reality for all believers. With Jesus living on the inside, the fruit of His Spirit will just happen.

Most of us experienced this reality in the beginning of our faith. I can remember accepting Jesus, and my heart was full of love for Him and other people. Joy was glowing inside. Peace was like a covering over me. I do not recall any Bible teacher having to tell me to feel these things. It was all just happening inside and it was tangible enough that I still smile when I think back about it. I knew it was there before I had any idea why. As I began to learn, I discovered it was the Holy Spirit taking up residency in my heart.

"The Spirit of God, who raised Jesus from the dead, lives in you. And just as God raised Christ Jesus from the dead, he will give life to your mortal bodies by this same Spirit living within you."

Romans 8:11 NLT

"And we have received God's Spirit (not the world's spirit), so we can know the wonderful things God has freely given us."

1 Corinthians 2:12 NLT

THE SPIRIT

As we discussed in chapter two, Jesus living inside of us is the source of joy. Circling back to it here may seem redundant but we also often need reminders. I find it important to remind myself that all good flows from the Holy Spirit, and He is already within me. If we are not careful, we get busy on these religious treadmills of routine, and the truth floats away like a birthday balloon escaping from a small child's hand. His Spirit produces the fruit of joy. If I find myself joyless as a believer, I can know instantly that, on some level, I am no longer walking in the light of His influence. I have lost sight of Jesus, or His Kingdom, or His love for me, or my place in His family. I am listening to the lies of the adversary as he whispers them through the fence, or the cross has been obscured and I no longer have His love and sacrifice in view. On some level, the influence of His Spirit for joy in my heart is being smothered by a competing lie or a deceptive distortion of my circumstances. The joy should be natural, which means that the lack of joy is what should instantly feel like an unnatural state for the child of God.

"So now we can rejoice in our wonderful new relationship with God because our Lord Jesus Christ has made us friends of God."

Romans 5:11 NLT

King David got himself in trouble many times over the course of his life. He was far from perfect, even though he had a heart to pursue and know the Lord. God had chosen him specifically to be the king and had instructed one of His greatest prophets, Samuel, to anoint him ruler of Israel. He won many victories for the Lord, but he also struggled against many inner iniquities that would persistently show up in his life. Psalms 51 is perhaps one of the most honest and transparent prayers recorded anywhere in the scripture. David was crying out from a broken place because he had sinned against the Lord again.

"Oh, give me back my joy again; you have broken me—now let me rejoice."

Psalms 51:8 NLT

"Restore to me the joy of your salvation, and make me willing to obey you."

Psalms 51:12 NLT

Even though David lived under the Old Covenant, we can still learn something valuable from his experience.

When our joy is gone, it means that something is wrong in our hearts.

It may not be some great sin. Lack of joy does not automatically mean God is angry with us and we are in danger of judgment. Struggling to find joy does not indicate a lack of God's love for us or that the devil is overpowering us. But we also should not simply accept it as the new normal and allow ourselves to follow Jesus without joy. When we notice joy missing, we should train ourselves to turn our faces back toward our Father instantly. In our places of prayer and communion with God, we find our vision restored, and all of these wonderful reminders we have been looking at come back into view. Stated simply, a lack of joy in the Lord should make us pray. And I'm not talking about prayer born out of some selfish need to feel better. It should be prayer that flows from an understanding that with the Holy Spirit living inside of me, joy should be abiding in my heart.

Make no mistake, if you are engaging in sin, it will destroy your joy in the Lord. Sinful decisions are like poison to a Christian. The deception at work that helps us make choices that dishonor God is always hiding this fact from us. Sin gently prods us and promises happiness and fulfillment of some desire we hold inside. This advertisement campaign for the darkness never includes the fine print that after the good time is over, our joy will be gone and our peace will be missing as well. David learned this from a place of personal failure that shook him to his core. In the moments of passion, his quest to commit adultery brought only anticipation of great sexual pleasure and conquest. When the dust settled, he was a broken man crying out to God in great awareness that his sin had nearly destroyed his relationship with the One Who loved him.

> *"Wash me clean from my guilt. Purify me from my sin. For I recognize my rebellion; it haunts me day and night. Against you, and you alone, have I sinned; I have done what is evil in your sight. You will be proved right in what you say, and your judgment against me is just."*
>
> *Psalms 51:2-4 NLT*

If you are reading this and sin has played its tricks on you, allow David's prayer to inform your own. Repent of your sin. Make no more excuses and submit to God's declarations of what is right and wrong, good and evil. See the evil you have chosen as the vile and unclean thing it is and throw it far from you. It was a lie that you could sin willfully and also walk with Christ. Your lack of joy proves that you may be putting on a good enough act for people around you, but you are grieving the heart of the Savior living within you. No matter who you manage to hide your sin from, Jesus is a firsthand witness to all of it. If He did not love you, He would not bother you over it. He loves you so much that your actions are painful to Him. We feel that pain as a *conviction* of our sin. The pathway back to joy is getting back on the path that pleases Jesus.

"Temptation comes from our own desires, which entice us and drag us away. These desires give birth to sinful actions. And when sin is allowed to grow, it gives birth to death."

James 1:14-15 NLT

Even when we are not entangled in sin, we can find ourselves lacking joy. The absence of it is still symptomatic of a soul problem. When our joy is gone because of sin, the answer is repentance. When our joy is gone for any other reason, the answer is remembrance. That is ultimately what this book is about.

I found that the key to *maintaining* my joy was reminding myself of the goodness of God. I find that the key to *restoring* my joy when it is gone is reminding myself of the goodness of God.

THE SPIRIT

In those times that I have chosen sin over sanctity, the answer was repentance and then reminding myself of the goodness of God. When we turn our eyes back toward the Word and the Kingdom, our constant companion and guide is the Holy Spirit. David knew this as well. He knew he could not get back without the help of the Spirit of God.

"Create in me a clean heart, O God. Renew a loyal spirit within me. Do not banish me from your presence, and don't take your Holy Spirit from me."

Psalms 51:10-11 NLT

David knew that no amount of human effort would restore his soul. He knew that if the Holy Spirit were to depart and leave him alone, he would never find his way back to God. We must always remember the same. Without the Holy Spirit we would have never come to faith in Christ to begin with. In the same way that the Spirit led us to eternal life with Jesus, He is now the One leading us to the forgotten truths and neglected paths that have allowed our joy to dwindle and die. The great news is that He is not far away. He is living inside the believer and continues making all things good available to us. Take a moment and thank God for the presence of His Spirit.

"For the Kingdom of God is not a matter of what we eat or drink, but of living a life of goodness and peace and joy in the Holy Spirit."

Romans 14:17 NLT

There are some very practical personal disciplines we can develop that are powerful because they help us get back in tune with His Spirit. That connection is what renews our minds and gives us liberty from lies and misconceptions.

We will never have more joy in our lives than our fellowship with Christ cultivates.

Joy is fruit, and fruit grows naturally if the conditions are right. With the right amount of *Son light*, and the *rain* of Living Water, the fruit of the Spirit can fill our lives. Learning to be *in the Spirit*, to *walk in the Spirit*, and to be *led by the Spirit* becomes the bridge that leads us back to our joy. The fruit of the Spirit has nothing to do with our circumstances in this world and everything to do with our relationship with Christ. There is a place in that relationship that is so healthy we can live out what Paul admonished us to.

"Always be joyful."

1 Thessalonians 5:16 NLT

In our culture driven by feelings, there is almost an instant response of justification for a lack of joy. We might make someone who lacks joy feel bad or less than someone else. Some would advise me to tread gently because I would not want to imply that the joyless are loved less by God. Some would demand that I stop right here to acknowledge that certain health conditions are beyond our control and can make it nearly impossible to have joy. But I would rather hold out the hope found in the Scripture. If you are wrestling with depression, you are loved, and God is good. Allow the truth spoken to us by our Creator to have more weight than the diagnosis you received from your physician. Your diagnosis is temporary. God's Word is eternal and true! His Spirit can nourish our lives until the fruit is flourishing, and His joy leaves no room for that depression.

"Oh, the joys of those who do not follow the advice of the wicked, or stand around with sinners, or join in with mockers. But they delight in the law of the Lord, meditating on it day and night. They are like trees planted along the riverbank, bearing fruit each season. Their leaves never wither, and they prosper in all they do."

Psalms 1:1-3 NLT

Meditation, in its original form, focused on a truth spoken by God and reminded us of it repeatedly while in prayer and fellowship with Him. He promises we will see a remarkable harvest that is enduring in all seasons if we can learn to do that. Pursue that level of relationship with Jesus. Seek fellowship with His Spirit throughout your day and set aside special times to focus and pray. Allow His light to fill your soul and rejoice in all that He reveals. As we do, the fruit He produces will become more and more prevalent in our lives. Allow the fruit of the Spirit to grow, and it will begin to change everything about your journey. You can see the fruit of joy and peace grow in your life until other people see it. You can see fruit grow in your life until what you need from your physician changes, and some of what they said about you is no longer true.

God actually modeled this for all of us prophetically in the Old Testament. Following a rebellion in the camp of

Israelites led by a man named Korah, the Lord instructed Moses to establish a principle of His divine selection to forever settle the question of who God had chosen for leadership. In Chapter 17 of Numbers, the Lord tells Moses to get a staff from each of the twelve leaders of the twelve tribes. He then inscribed that leader's name upon his staff. Then the Lord gave this instruction:

> *"Place these staffs in the Tabernacle in front of the Ark containing the tablets of the Covenant, where I meet with you. Buds will sprout on the staff belonging to the man I choose. Then I will finally put an end to the people's murmuring and complaining against you."*
>
> Numbers 17:4-5 NLT

Think about this for a moment because it is significant. A staff is a branch from a tree that is dead. When you cut it down and then carry it around, the wood dries out, and the ability to bear fruit is forever lost. All twelve staffs were dead wood. All twelve were placed before the Ark where God met with Moses. The Lord declared that He would reveal who was chosen by fruitfulness returning to their dead branch. When we consider all the ways God could have settled this dispute, we are forced to conclude that fruitfulness must be significant to the Lord.

> *"When he went into the Tabernacle of the Covenant the next day, he found that Aaron's staff, representing the tribe of Levi, had sprouted, budded, blossomed, and produced ripe almonds!"*
>
> Numbers 17:8 NLT

THE SPIRIT

The dead staff produced fruit! God uses the fruit to indicate the one He had chosen. The Lord provides this clear lesson that who He has chosen will bear fruit. The dead stick comes back to life. When God chooses, it brings life, and the evidence of that life is shown through the fruit it bears. This lesson was so important to the Lord that He commanded that the staff be forever preserved as a sign to all generations who would follow the Ark.

"And the Lord said to Moses: 'Place Aaron's staff permanently before the Ark of the Covenant to serve as a warning to rebels. This should put an end to their complaints against me and prevent further deaths.' So Moses did as the Lord commanded him."

Numbers 17:10-11 NLT

When you consider what happened here, it directly applies to what we have been looking at in this chapter. The rod of Aaron only produced fruit because it spent time in the presence of the Lord. His rod was allowed to rest in the place where God had chosen to meet with Moses. In that place of communion and fellowship, the dead branch bears fruit once again. It was literally the *fruit of the Spirit*! There was no soil, no water, and nobody tending it. Only a few hours of time passed, and those hours were dark. The fruit was a miracle because no natural path was available for this staff to produce fruit. The only factor involved was God's Spirit and presence there in the tent of meeting. From that meeting place, fruit began to grow. It is a powerful reminder to every believer that the *fruit* of the Spirit grows from fellowship with the Lord and not religious efforts.

If we want the dead areas of our lives to bear fruit again, we need to abide with Jesus and make a priority of our fellowship time with Him.

In that place of meeting, the eternal life of the Kingdom of God begins to give life to our mortal bodies. All the fruit of the Spirit begins to grow there. The light is His love and presence. The water is His Spirit. The nutrients flow from the eternal truths of His Word. The more we abide, the more we grow. Joy is just one aspect of this. The path to joy is also the path to more love, peace, kindness, faithfulness, and self-control. That path leads to times of regular fellowship with Christ. When I look back over my walk of faith, it is abundantly clear to me that when I have made a priority of my time with Jesus, it is evident in my life. The evidence is the *fruit* described in Galatians. I am kinder, and when things go wrong, I am gentler. When my old nature tries to make an appearance, it is easier for me to control it. When I have allowed myself to get careless or inconsistent with my devotion time, more of the old me starts to reveal itself. The *fruit of the Spirit* is truly *fruit* that grows from time with His Spirit. If we want to walk in our joy, we will have to put effort into guarding that time and keeping our meetings with Jesus.

THE SPIRIT

CHAPTER NINE REFLECTION QUESTIONS

"The third person of the Trinity."

1. How do many Christians view the list of the fruit of the Spirit in Galatians?
2. What are your earliest memories of the effects of the indwelling Holy Spirit on your life and emotions upon accepting Christ as your Savior?
3. How do you respond to the statement "Lacking joy should instantly feel like an unnatural state"?
4. What observations can you make when considering the statement "We will never have more joy in our lives than our fellowship with Christ cultivates"?
5. What role can meditation upon the scripture play in your spiritual health and well-being?
6. What lesson can we all take away from the budding of Aaron's rod in Numbers 17?

———

"Praise is the mode of love which always
has some element of joy in it."

—C.S. Lewis

CHAPTER TEN

THE SONGS

"You have turned my mourning into joyful dancing. You have taken away my clothes of mourning and clothed me with joy, that I might sing praises to you and not be silent. O Lord my God, I will give you thanks forever!"

Psalms 30:11-12 NLT

Our worship plays an important role in our soul. When we fix our eyes upon the Lord, we take our eyes off ourselves. Everything about Him fills us with joy because He is perfect in all of His ways. Almost everything weighing us down with regrets and worries is magnified when we keep our focus on ourselves. My focus determines a huge amount of my experience. True worship will always bring life into our spirit because we are looking into the face of our Redeemer, and He is the Resurrection and the Life. In worship, we are reminded of all the amazing aspects of grace, love, and mercy that we have been reminding ourselves of with this study. Worship is a close companion of the meditation we discussed in the last chapter, and meditation brings fruitfulness to our lives. Our decision to offer our worship to God represents a sacrifice we are making to Him. We are offering our time and our energy, and we are humbling ourselves. All of this pleases the Lord and can lead to amazing moments of fellowship with Him.

"Therefore, let us offer through Jesus a continual sacrifice of praise to God, proclaiming our allegiance to his name."

Hebrews 13:15 NLT

Worship through music has been a revolution that has impacted almost every corner of the modern church. Even denominations that were resistant have slowly embraced it. The Western church is brimming with talented worship leaders and songwriters. A good offering of musical worship is now a part of nearly every Christian gathering, no matter what name is on the sign out front. We have never had more opportunities to sing praises to God. Streaming channels and radio stations are dedicated to Christian music artists' creations. All of it sounds wonderful. On top of all that, the internet gives us a doorway into hundreds of congregations as they gather and sing. Worship is everywhere! Or is it?

Worship is not exempt from our human failing of lacking fidelity.

We are very capable of divergent motivations that cause little harmony between our outward actions and our inward affections. Stated simply, we are all able to be fake. This is no surprise to the God Who formed us and then watched as we yielded to the influence of sin. He has observed this throughout human history. He also consistently calls His people to rise above this disingenuous instinct. Jesus states this desire in very clear terms.

> "But the time is coming—indeed it's here now—when true worshipers will worship the Father in spirit and in truth. The Father is looking for those who will worship him that way."
>
> John 4:23 NLT

Jesus declares a volume of truth in this one statement. All that is revealed here is worth our daily consideration as modern followers of His. When music is everywhere, naturally stimulating our emotions, and everything is designed to engineer an experience, we do well to heed His instruction.

Jesus starts with the fact that there are true and false worshipers.

The activity of a worship service is no guarantee of the truth of the worshipers in that gathering. In a season when our leaders are willing to help us engage in religious-looking practices, the appearance of the crowd is no longer a reliable measure of what is happening. Turn off the sound and you cannot see any difference between the large worship gathering and the concert happening down the street. Merely attending such an event is not worshiping in truth.

True worshipers worship the Father according to Jesus. Declaring the worth of our God is the starting point of our worship. He is the One we are looking at, and He is the

One we are impressed with. His perfection is what we express our admiration for. We celebrate His love and grace. His truth and eternal goodness become the source of our songs. Worship is about Him. Even if that seems obvious, turn the sound off again and read the lyrics of many modern worship anthems. You will notice many well-known songs are about us and not about Him.

Worship in spirit and in truth is the next aspect that Jesus teaches as important to our God. This gets to the heart of the issue because it is God looking at our hearts as we worship. We raise our hands, and He looks at our spirit. We sing our songs, and He looks at our spirit. We clap our hands, and He is still looking at our spirit. He looks past our video screens and the graphics they display. He looks beyond our posture and our presentation. He listens deeper than our practiced harmonies and perfect chord progressions. He looks for those who worship in spirit and truth.

The wording is deeper than people see on the surface. Most read it and think instantly that truth is a reference to the Bible and the spirit refers to their personal appraisal of what the Holy Spirit is doing in the moment. In reality, Jesus is speaking of fidelity and consistency within the lives of the worshipers. Worship in spirit involves our whole being responding to Who He is. Worship, in truth, is the challenge for our entire being to reflect honest love and admiration for God. God looks for us to mean what we sing while our spirit, soul, and body are functioning as one unified sacrifice of praise.

THE SONGS

"These people honor me with their lips, but their hearts are far from me."

Matthew 15:8 NLT

This statement came from the prophet Isaiah and was later quoted by Jesus in rebuking the scribes and Pharisees. We can all relate to this precarious situation if we are honest with ourselves. We clap our hands to the drums while we analyze what someone else is wearing. We sing the familiar words while rehearsing an earlier conversation in our minds. We blend into the crowd and respond appropriately on cue even when our minds are entirely engaged elsewhere. This is not worship *in spirit and in truth*. When this becomes our habit, we are once again going through religious motions rather than having true fellowship with Christ. Only true fellowship brings the life of the Spirit of God into our hearts.

Standing in a gathering of worshipers and watching will never resurrect your joy. Joy is in His presence, and the pathway to His presence is worship *in spirit and in truth*. Our opportunities to worship with the family of faith should be fueling our souls with joy every time we offer God our praise. Do you remember where we started this discussion? Before I could explain anything about my faith, I was finding joy in His presence, singing simple songs in that little church. The reason is now obvious: I truly meant every word with all of my being. I was worshiping *in spirit and in truth*! What changed over time was that religious routines had "helped me" learn to act like I was worshiping on the outside with my heart somewhere else. I had acquired the skill of being disingenuous. My focus had shifted from God to me. There is a solid chance this has happened to you as well. We believe that we *worship* God simply because we attend a church where worship music happens. There is no joy to be found in that falsehood.

Does the reality of Who God is still inspire you with awe and wonder? Be honest with yourself because it is easy to learn how to act inspired and yet have our hearts be focused somewhere else completely. When you consider the Creator of everything, does it make you pause and think? If the secular humanism in our culture fills your mind, you will lose your wonder and this whole existence becomes some great cosmic accident. Does the memory of Jesus, our Savior, hanging in agony on the cross to cover our sins warm your heart with gratitude? If the humanists cloud your thinking, Christianity becomes nothing more than a personal preference and a box to be checked on a survey. Do you long for the wind of the Spirit as on the day of Pentecost? Listen to enough online critics and you will lose that longing and regard everyone who still possesses that longing with cynicism. When your mind turns the pages back to your own conversion, does it stop you as worship fills your heart? If we allow religious routines to become our expression of choice, that desire to lift up holy hands and bless Him will be slowly replaced with a detached church performance routine.

One of the surest pathways to consistent and sustained joy in the Lord is becoming a *spirit and truth* worshiper again! See your entire being as a sacrifice you are able to bring to Jesus over and over again. Like the fires on the altar burning perpetually in the Old Testament Tabernacle, let your praise rise to God every morning and every evening. Cultivate the

THE SONGS

ability to worship when you are all alone. Cultivate the ability to worship driving in your car rather than just listening to music. Learn to declare the praises of God. Read the Psalms and stop at every line, declaring it as your own. Learn to sing the praises of God, whether you feel like you have a great voice or not. Study the various postures of worship, like raising your hands and kneeling down, and make them all part of your personal times with God. Most of all, keep your focus on God. This is not about you or how you feel in the moment. This is all about Him! It's about how much He loves you and then displayed that love for the world to see when He sent Jesus to the cross. This is about Jesus obeying the Father and willingly taking your place so you did not have to die in payment for your own sin. This is about the Holy Spirit gently pulling you home to the Father. Embrace all of that, and then lift your arms and hands and voice, and worship God *in spirit and in truth*.

CHAPTER TEN REFLECTION QUESTIONS

"Then sings my soul."

1. If you consider your worship a sacrifice, how does that affect your decision to praise the Lord?
2. What changes have you observed in your church experiences as the worship music revolution has occurred in recent years?
3. What is your reaction to the statement that there are true and false worshipers?
4. Why do you think it is so easy for most of us to *honor God* with our words while our *hearts are far* from Him?
5. What steps can you take right now to bring personal worship into your quiet times with Jesus?

"True joy comes not when we pursue our own greatness, but when we lay down our lives for the sake of others."

—Francis Chan

CHAPTER ELEVEN

THE TOWEL

> *"Oh, praise the Lord, all you servants of the Lord, you who serve at night in the house of the Lord. Lift your hands toward the sanctuary, and praise the Lord."*
>
> Psalms 134:1-2 NLT

In the sanctuary of the Lord there was continual activity to ensure the various lamps were burning, the incense was rising, and the atmosphere was guarded and holy. Twenty-four hours a day, seven days per week, the duties of the Tabernacle were the number one priority of everyone serving there. They planned their lives around their service to God by maintaining the worship of the sanctuary. If you were given this privilege, you did not randomly take a sick day or get too busy to show up. The high call was to simply serve there, and this service was regarded with honor. The writer of this Psalms is encouraging those who serve by night to do it with worship in their hearts and praise on their lips.

Those who served during the day could be seen as they went about their assignments. Those serving at night had almost no human audience.

Serving at night was done in the sight of God rather than the sight of men. There was no need to appear more spiritual or consecrated to impress the onlookers. The only One watching was God. With an audience of One, they performed their sacred duties and honored the God of Heaven by serving Him according to His expressed desires. It is awesome to imagine that environment and how wonderful the presence of the Lord must have been; tremendous unseen power surging from behind the veil as the lamps flickered over the table of bread. Imagine serving there and being constantly aware that your nation was chosen by God and set apart as sacred. Your tribe was chosen. Your family was chosen. You had been chosen to serve the Creator of all things! These tasks were not mundane, repetitious nonsense. Each one was a privilege because of Who was being served.

This system of worship was the central construct in the Jewish audience that Jesus was teaching about during His earthly ministry. He referenced their understanding over and over as He worked to get them moving toward the new thing God was doing. It was a New Covenant that He was establishing with His own blood. It was a transfer of setting as the God behind the veil moved out of the Holy of Holies and into the hearts of every man and woman who would believe. With dramatic emphasis, He would rip the veil Himself to tell the world that the space was no longer holy because He was moving into new temples. The people He created would now be able to carry His presence because their sin would be wiped away!

Jesus spoke most clearly about this when teaching His disciples, preparing them to become the leaders of the new Church He was establishing. Do you remember this statement?

"If you love me, obey my commandments. And I will ask the Father, and he will give you another Advocate, who will never leave you. He is the Holy Spirit, who leads into all truth. The world cannot receive him, because it isn't looking for him and doesn't recognize him. But you know him, because he lives with you now and later will be in you."

John 14:15-17 NLT

The indwelling presence of God's Spirit is the key to everything. The Kingdom is now within us and the presence of God is among us. Rather than abiding in one small place, He has cleansed and purified millions of hearts and souls and dwells within us. The Apostle Paul taught diligently to help the Gentile part of the Church catch up to what the Jewish part already understood.

"Don't you realize that your body is the temple of the Holy Spirit, who lives in you and was given to you by God?"

1 Corinthians 6:19 NLT

He wanted each individual believer to understand that Christ was moving in. He was occupying the temple of their life. His presence meant sacred separation and holiness for every person calling themself a Christian. He also wanted the local church to understand the corporate worship dynamic of this abiding presence.

"Together, we are his house, built on the foundation of the apostles and the prophets. And the cornerstone is Christ Jesus himself. We are carefully joined together in him, becoming a holy temple for the Lord. Through him you Gentiles are also being made part of this dwelling where God lives by his Spirit."

Ephesians 2:20-22 NLT

A true believer standing anywhere in the world is a temple for the God of Heaven. Two or three such believers gathering together anywhere in the world form a dwelling place for God by His Spirit. A larger gathering just becomes a larger temple that is holy and set apart for God. The Jewish believers had a point of reference for all of this because of their tabernacle history with worship. But they struggled to truly grasp the wonder of it because the temple had always been regarded as so incredibly holy that they dared not approach that space behind the veil. The Gentile believers struggled with all of it. The idea of only one God was revolutionary. Their world was full of temples and tabernacles to every conceivable kind of god and deity. But they did understand that the temple for any god was the sacred space that belonged to that god. Paul was trying to get them to realize that now they were the sacred space that belonged to the true God.

"For we are both God's workers. And you are God's field. You are God's building."

1 Corinthians 3:9 NLT

THE TOWEL

The realization that a gathering of Christians constitutes the House of God is profound! Just as the Tabernacle of old journeyed through the desert during 40 years of wandering, we now establish a new Tabernacle whenever and wherever we come together to worship God. This Tabernacle appears in living rooms and basements, in sanctuaries adorned with stained glass, in rented storefronts next to pizza shops, in arena-sized mega ministries, and on back porches filled with singing voices. God has moved out of a single holy place and now resides within each of us, made holy by the cleansing power of the blood of Jesus. We are His sanctuary.

> *"Oh, praise the Lord, all you servants of the Lord, you who serve at night in the house of the Lord. Lift your hands toward the sanctuary, and praise the Lord."*
>
> Psalms 134:1-2 NLT

How do we *serve at night in the house of the Lord* if the house is gone? If any believer we encounter is the temple of the Holy Spirit, how would we serve there? If any gathering of believers is the House of God, how would we serve there? The answer from Jesus is quite simple.

We serve God in His sanctuary by serving one another!

On the night of the Last Supper, Jesus made this the primary point of His final teachings before the crucifixion. He had just explained the covenant change that was taking place. He had shocked everyone by announcing the betrayal that was to come. Their shock triggered an argument about importance. Who among all of them would be the greatest in the new Kingdom? Jesus interrupts their argument with a startling declaration.

"Jesus told them, 'In this world the kings and great men lord it over their people, yet they are called 'friends of the people.' But among you it will be different. Those who are the greatest among you should take the lowest rank, and the leader should be like a servant. Who is more important, the one who sits at the table or the one who serves? The one who sits at the table, of course. But not here! For I am among you as one who serves.'"

Luke 22:25-27 NLT

Just when the group could not have been more perplexed, the scripture tells us what happened next.

"So he got up from the table, took off his robe, wrapped a towel around his waist, and poured water into a basin. Then he began to wash the disciples' feet, drying them with the towel he had around him."

John 13:4-5 NLT

Tradition holds that it was the household slave's role to wash visitor's feet. Jesus had told them plainly that to serve others is the way forward in His new Kingdom. He then illustrates it in a way that would have truly shaken His disciples. They called Him Master. They often called Him Lord. They had seen His miracles and listened to His teachings. They had witnessed Him rebuking demons and raging seas. They had given up everything to follow Him because they believed He was the future King. Yet here He is at their feet.

THE TOWEL

> *"When Jesus came to Simon Peter, Peter said to him, 'Lord, are you going to wash my feet?' Jesus replied, 'You don't understand now what I am doing, but someday you will.' 'No,' Peter protested, 'you will never wash my feet!'"*
>
> John 13:6-8 NLT

This outburst by Peter gives us a glimpse into how unthinkable this was to them. Every part of them must have screamed internally, "This is wrong!" The Master deserves honor and royalty. They did not realize that in a few hours, Jesus would be far more humiliated by the Roman soldiers and King Herod than the shame He was choosing now. He was simply taking the lowest rank as He was instructing them to do.

> *"After washing their feet, he put on his robe again and sat down and asked, 'Do you understand what I was doing? You call me 'Teacher' and 'Lord,' and you are right, because that's what I am. And since I, your Lord and Teacher, have washed your feet, you ought to wash each other's feet. I have given you an example to follow. Do as I have done to you. I tell you the truth, slaves are not greater than their master. Nor is the messenger more important than the one who sends the message. Now that you know these things, God will bless you for doing them."*
>
> John 13:12-17 NLT

With one powerful illustrated sermon, He called all of His followers to take that lowest rank and humbly serve one another like house slaves. When our pride is aroused by this concept, He reminds us that messengers are not more important than the One who sends them. We are the messengers sent out with the Gospel. He is the One sending us. If He can wash feet, we are left with no excuse other than our own sin and selfishness if we refuse to serve in lowly ways. Others are His house and we are called to serve God in His house.

The Apostle Paul realized this and made it his life's mission.

> *"Even though I am a free man with no master, I have become a slave to all people to bring many to Christ."*
>
> *1 Corinthians 9:19 NLT*

Have you ever wondered how Paul achieved all that he did? He planted numerous churches. He wrote the majority of the New Testament. He endured amazing hardships and difficulties. Many of his journeys were tumultuous and challenging. Several people betrayed him and some that he relied on failed him miserably. How did he do that? He regarded every aspect of it as service in God's house! Nothing difficult he was forced to walk through was beneath him because he was just a slave of the House of God. His service was to God alone and he was willing to labor by night for an audience of One. His assigned tasks in the house were some of the most difficult, and he moved about the house, serving frequently with very little help. His eyes were on the Lord, and he refused to waiver from serving Him. He was living life with a towel in his hands.

> *"Oh, praise the Lord, all you servants of the Lord, you who serve at night in the house of the Lord. Lift your hands toward the sanctuary, and praise the Lord."*
>
> *Psalms 134:1-2 NLT*

If you're not convinced that being a servant was Paul's primary focus, I encourage you to look at how he opened his letters.

> "This letter is from Paul, a slave of Christ Jesus, chosen by God to be an apostle and sent out to preach his Good News."
>
> Romans 1:1 NLT

> "This letter is from Paul and Timothy, slaves of Christ Jesus."
>
> Philippians 1:1 NLT

> "This letter is from Paul, a slave of God and an apostle of Jesus Christ."
>
> Titus 1:1

He clearly understood the nature of this new Kingdom. He understood that serving Jesus was the ultimate expression of devotion to Jesus. He also understood that serving Jesus meant serving other people because they were the House of God. Because his perspective was the *lowest rank* he did not lose heart when he was treated like *the lowest rank*. He was brilliant, highly educated, and capable of standing tall in front of any philosopher. He had seen the miraculous power of the Holy Spirit flow through his life and produce mighty signs and wonders in front of his own eyes. Rather than look for service from others, his focus was serving God more fully by serving as many of God's people as he could. He, like Jesus, modeled it for everyone to see.

> "Don't you remember, dear brothers and sisters, how hard we worked among you? Night and day we toiled to earn a living

so that we would not be a burden to any of you as we preached God's Good News to you."

1 Thessalonians 2:9 NLT

When so many in our day leverage any amount of ministry success into more honor for themselves, we see the great apostle refusing to stop working. His focus was the people and serving the Lord by selflessly serving them. In the book of Acts, we find that he often worked as a tent maker. This was a physically demanding job when a person was healthy. With years of injury and abuse for the sake of the Kingdom, Paul would no doubt have endured great struggles to work like this, and yet he would not have it any other way. How did he do it? He saw every hot afternoon sewing canvas as service in the House of God. Every late evening of teaching the people and praying for the sick was honorable service in the House of God. Hunger or pain did not dissuade him. He was not moved by threats or false arrests. He was living every day with a towel of service in his hands.

If this book is about joy, why are we talking about serving? Everyone knows that serving is the ugly part of all this. Serving is the sacrifice that we make without any expectation in return. We put a smile on our face, do our Christian duty, and then breathe easier as soon as it is over. There is an obligation to do those things that look Christian. Should we expect any joy from that? The answer depends entirely on who we are serving.

"Work with enthusiasm, as though you are working for the Lord rather than for people."

Ephesians 6:7 NLT

THE TOWEL

"Work willingly at whatever you do, as though you were working for the Lord rather than for people."

Colossians 3:23 NLT

My experience has been that if I keep my focus on Jesus, I find joy in serving Him. Conversely, if I allow my focus to shift to the people and how they respond to my service, I can quickly become discouraged and find it all to be nothing more than work. Remember that phrase, *servants of the Lord*, we keep recalling? Say it one word at a time. Servants. Of. The. Lord. *Servant* becomes my identity. *Of* reveals my focus as being the Lord. *The* reminds me that there is only One God to serve. *Lord* reminds me of Who I am serving. The people are His house, but the house is His! To serve Him in His house requires that my focus be on Him instead of them. Paul knew this and admonished the Gentile believers to serve with their eyes on Jesus. This really does transform what happens inside of us as we serve.

When I think back to the happy guy who was leading the singing at my first church, I realize that he was always happy because he was singing *to Jesus*. Sometimes, the people sang along with enthusiasm. Other times, they appeared dull and lifeless. One weekend, the piano player was *in the zone*, and it sounded wonderful. The next Sunday, the right chords were not even on the page. The sound was good one week and then blessing us all with feedback the next. The squeaky air conditioner on the old roof would keep us cool one day and then seem to pump heat into the building the next. Amidst all those shifting circumstances, the happy guy was just looking happy. With a smile across his face, he would sing song after song, rejoicing in the Lord. It was like the rest of us were not even there. This brings us back to the word *focus*. When you focus on anything, the things around it become blurry and less defined.

Focus on Jesus and we see Him clearly, and the others— attitudes and all—lose definition. That is the key to finding joy in serving.

A great number of service opportunities are *at night,* which just means they are unwitnessed by the crowd. One of the driving factors in the shrinking number of willing servants in local congregations is that too many only want to serve in areas in the light of day. They desire to be seen serving. They desire the platform and the podium. They crave the appreciation and value the compliments of the people. They are not as attracted to the *lowest rank* that Jesus was modeling. Sadly, they miss the joy of serving *with* Jesus in His house. They miss the fellowship we have with Him when we focus on Him and make His desires our priorities. Working with Jesus cultivates a joy that is entirely missed by those who merely attend church and listen to information about Him.

When Paul was sharing his heart with one church he had planted, he enlightened us with his perspective on serving the Lord, laboring in the gospel, and finding joy in it.

> *"After all, what gives us hope and joy, and what will be our proud reward and crown as we stand before our Lord Jesus when he returns? It is you! Yes, you are our pride and joy."*
>
> 1 Thessalonians 2:19-20 NLT

THE TOWEL

Serving the Lord aligns us with His will and positions us to see His Kingdom working on this earth! It can be difficult and discouraging. Our strength can wax and wane and our faith can be shaken. As we keep our eyes on Him and His return, we also see His workmanship in people's lives. We will never see all that we desire to see, but we will see the Word of God planted, cultivated, and bearing fruit in other lives. We will realize that our efforts, even if hidden from human spectators, are seen by our Father and become a part of His plan unfolding around us. Live with a towel in your hand. Take the *lowest rank* and serve the Lord in His house. You will be following the example set by Jesus, and He promised a blessing on every person who will trust Him and take up their towel.

CHAPTER ELEVEN REFLECTION QUESTIONS

"Washing some dirty feet."

1. How does the idea that *every true believer is a sacred place where God is dwelling* impact how you view other followers of Jesus?

2. In what way is serving another believer also serving the Lord?

3. Why do you think Peter initially refused to have Jesus wash his feet?

4. How does your heart respond to the teaching of Jesus that taking the lowest place and serving others is the pathway to Kingdom progress?

5. How is it possible for acts of service done for others to produce joy in our own lives?

6. How important is our focus when we are serving others?

"The happiest moments of a Christian's life are when he sits at the Lord's Table and feels the joy of full redemption."

—Charles Spurgeon

CHAPTER TWELVE

THE MEAL

Looking back over my journey, I find that some of the most meaningful conversations and impartations happened in homes rather than church sanctuaries or convention halls. When I first came to Jesus, that precious family took me in, and they discipled me. The *happy singing guy* was my first spiritual mentor. Sitting at his table, we spent hours reading scriptures, while he explained all that he had learned along the way. Those conversations were formative. There is something so authentic and tangible about talking around the dinner table. I think it is because there is no planned presentation happening there. It is a dialogue rather than the monologue that sermons turn into. Every aspect of it teaches you something about the faith and understanding of your host. Your questions are allowed, and learning is the result. We lose sight of the fact that for centuries, the house was the meeting place of the church, and the owner of the house was typically the *elder* of that portion of the local church.

> *"I am writing to Philemon, our beloved co-worker, and to our sister Apphia, and to our fellow soldier Archippus, and to the church that meets in your house."*
>
> *Philemon 1-2 NLT*

The Last Supper was more of a house meal with teaching than a ceremony or church ritual. Because of the importance of what happened there, it was inevitable that it would be reflected in the liturgy and practice of the church. Do not lose sight of the original setting. A simple room with no statues or stained glass. A gathering of friends and followers who were walking together into this new mission for Christ. It was a simple setting for a profound message.

In the previous chapter, we explored the emphasis Jesus placed during His final hours on *serving* one another.

He illustrated His own message in a powerful way when He took up the towel and washed all of their dirty feet.

But again, we must understand the original and simple setting for this. It would not have been a decorated golden laver inscribed with scriptures. A wooden bowl and clay vessel were the tools of this moment. We know that Jesus dressed so plainly that He could vanish into the crowd at any moment because there was nothing noteworthy about His attire. We can be certain He did not suddenly don a large and elaborate ecclesiastical robe. Everything about it was everyday appropriate. The Son of God was expressing the Kingdom of God in the same setting He had chosen many times during the

THE MEAL

previous three years: a simple house. In a simple house, He broke the bread and poured the wine and committed the Last Supper to those who would follow Him.

> *"He took some bread and gave thanks to God for it. Then he broke it in pieces and gave it to the disciples, saying, "This is my body, which is given for you. Do this in remembrance of me."*
>
> *Luke 22:19 NLT*

We have already discussed the human failure to slip into ritual and lose the meaning behind the origin of the ritual. We have explored the fact that we can appear to worship outwardly while our hearts are far away. We are able to sit and appear to listen to Bible teaching without actually hearing it. Religion whispers in our ear that God is being *served* when we pretend in His Name, but the reality is quite different. God is served when we worship *in spirit and truth*. He is served when we truly receive His Word and yield our hearts to it. He is served when we honor His wishes and actually serve one another outside of church. When His desires become our priorities, we are truly following Him. The precious rite of communion is so often a mindless ritual that very few draw joy from it. With a little practice, we can receive the *cup and the cracker* and our hearts be as distant as they were during the worship music. This is because we fail to do the one thing Jesus commanded: remember.

We should all see the communion ritual as another aspect of our worship and approach it in *spirit and truth*.

A powerful thing happens when we fully engage in what Jesus intended. Communion embraced correctly is shifting our focus back to Jesus and helping us once again *fix our eyes on Him.*

"Therefore, since we are surrounded by such a huge crowd of witnesses to the life of faith, let us strip off every weight that slows us down, especially the sin that so easily trips us up. And let us run with endurance the race God has set before us. We do this by keeping our eyes on Jesus, the champion who initiates and perfects our faith. Because of the joy awaiting him, he endured the cross, disregarding its shame. Now he is seated in the place of honor beside God's throne."

Hebrews 12:1-2 NLT

An opportunity to partake of communion is a setting for restored joy in the Lord! We are purposefully turning our attention back to Christ and His sacrifice. In doing that, we are reminded of His love and the power of His mercy. We are reminded that He endured all of that so you and I could be redeemed and come to His table for dinner. We can find joy rising when we take communion if we slow down and deny the ritual impulse inside of us. Paul corrected misconduct around the setting of the communion meal and he challenged everyone to pause and search their heart before doing anything else.

"So anyone who eats this bread or drinks this cup of the Lord unworthily is guilty of sinning against the body and blood of the Lord. That is why you should examine yourself before eating the bread and drinking the cup."

1 Corinthians 11:27-28 NLT

THE MEAL

There have been hundreds of wonderful teachings about the full implications of this verse. My focus today is not examining any of those concepts but rather the broader admonition. *Before* we take communion, we should stop and examine ourselves. The existence of the instruction immediately helps us see that this is important for the believer. It matters how we approach this sacred meal that Jesus initiated. Jesus told us that the goal of the sacrament was to provide an opportunity for us to *remember* Him. He was already aware that as the church continued forward from that moment, we would be inclined to slip into mindless ritual rather than true moments of remembrance and worship. The value of this further unfolds when He tells us to do this often. Our Savior instructs us to take time and truly remember Him and His sacrifice for us, on a very consistent basis. The concept is a purposeful turning of our mind and heart back to Jesus and away from whatever else has occupied that space in our lives.

"Remember the things I have done in the past. For I alone am God! I am God, and there is none like me."

Isaiah 46:9 NLT

"I remember the days of old. I ponder all your great works and think about what you have done."

Psalms 143:5 NLT

"Let all that I am praise the Lord; may I never forget the good things he does for me."

Psalms 103:2 NLT

Our joy so often fades because we forget the source and the reason for our rejoicing. Every communion sacrament is an invitation to reject this inward spiritual degradation and renew our hearts again in the wonder of our God's love for us. The styles vary but, in some manner or another, we end up holding bread in our hands that represents Jesus allowing Himself to be broken so that God could make us whole. We end up tasting of a cup that testifies to His willingness to wash our sins away and make us new. If we engage fully in this moment, we find ourselves standing once again at the foot of the cross and gazing up at our Redeemer as He makes the ultimate sacrifice to set us free from sin and death! His love is on display there. From that place, the mercy and forgiveness of God flow out for the washing of all mankind. Everything about that restores our joy.

"Oh, what joy for those whose disobedience is forgiven, whose sins are put out of sight. Yes, what joy for those whose record the Lord has cleared of sin."

Romans 4:7-8 NLT

When you began reading this, you most likely did not say within yourself that the path back to joy would have to include regularly taking communion. That is what religion has done to us. It is time for every believer to pull the beauty and wonder of this sacred meal up out of the heap of empty rituals and allow the light of the truth to shine on it again. In the light of truth, it is a radiant and wonderful expression of worship and reminds us of love, mercy, and forgiveness in ways that should send us on our way rejoicing. We need to

THE MEAL

see each sacrament as a gift given to us by God. It is the gift of remembering what is eternal and important and allowing what is not to fade away. Each time, the joy of the Lord will rise again within us. Each time we are reminded, we reconnect with the wonder of His Kingdom and the eternal reality of the redemption we find in Christ.

"No, you have come to Mount Zion, to the city of the living God, the heavenly Jerusalem, and to countless thousands of angels in a joyful gathering. You have come to the assembly of God's firstborn children, whose names are written in heaven. You have come to God himself, who is judge over all things. You have come to the spirits of the righteous ones in heaven who have now been made perfect. You have come to Jesus, the one who mediates the new covenant between God and people, and to the sprinkled blood, which speaks of forgiveness instead of crying out for vengeance like the blood of Abel."

Hebrews 12:22-24 NLT

CHAPTER TWELVE REFLECTION QUESTIONS

"Break the bread and pour the wine."

1. How do you respond to the statement, "When His desires become our priorities, we are truly following Him"?
2. What is the one aspect of the Lord's Supper that is both essential and easy to overlook?
3. How powerful is the act of truly remembering what the Lord has done?
4. What is available to us in taking communion that has the potential to restore our joy in knowing Christ?
5. Would you consider making a decision to partake in the Lord's Supper alone as part of your private devotions?

"The truest, purest joy flows from a discovery of Jesus Christ. He is the hidden treasure that gives such joy to the finder."

—Robert Murray M'Cheyne

CHAPTER THIRTEEN

THE SECRET PLACE

> *"Joyful are those who obey his laws and search for him with all their hearts."*
>
> Psalms 119:2 NLT

In stark contrast to the religious routines that erode our joy, a wonderful relationship is available to us in Christ. Those routines do not represent participation in the relationship that God has called us to. In the natural, no rational person would suggest that reading a book about the moon is the same as walking there. To study and memorize the specifications of a wealthy person's home is no substitute for a dinner invitation from them. Standing and staring for hours at a vivid photograph of a grizzly bear is not the same as coming face to face with one on a hunting trail. Experience is more life-changing than information. Information may give us the guidance to have the experience, but once we experience it, all the information moves from theory to fact.

I once followed a small map down a trail in search of a waterfall. It was truly a journey of faith as I took each step based on the information I held in my hand. I was trusting the person who provided the information. At one point, I passed a person returning from the falls, and they reported it was amazing. Now I had a witness to the view telling me about it, and that made it easier for me to continue by faith. As good as the map and the testimony had been, stepping from the path onto the rocky ledge over the roaring river changed everything. I could feel the vibrations in the stones and the cool mist drifting up and resting on my arms. There were sights and sounds and smells. I could have told anyone about the waterfall before I saw it, based on reading the map. Now I could witness it firsthand and share with others the reality of experiencing those falls.

To experience Jesus is the reality of the Christian faith.

He is not a concept or an opinion. He is not a mindset or a preference. He is alive and dwelling within all true believers. His light reveals the path before us and the hidden sin within us. His love touches our hearts and moves us to touch this world. His truth is the foundation under our feet as well as the judge of our desires and appetites. The *information* of the Gospel points us in His direction. Others who have experienced His mercy then *witness* that it is good and life-changing. Neither of these things is a substitute for falling face-first into the rivers of God's grace. In that moment, the theories become facts, and the basis of our reality shifts toward His

THE SECRET PLACE

Kingdom. We are never the same again. The precious miracle of our salvation positions us for a vibrant relationship with God rather than a life-long ritual merely about Him.

"We proclaim to you what we ourselves have actually seen and heard so that you may have fellowship with us. And our fellowship is with the Father and his Son, Jesus Christ."

1 John 1:3 NLT

Consider for a moment the man who wrote these words. The Apostle John was the youngest of the original twelve disciples. He always positioned himself as close to Jesus as he could. Following the crucifixion, he was entrusted with the care of Mary, the mother of Jesus. His life was one of service and sacrifice as he proclaimed the Kingdom for decades. He was often the target of intense persecution. History suggests that the authorities attempted to kill him more than once. Despite all this conflict, he outlived all the others and was still faithfully serving Jesus and His Church, into his old age. When the Romans could not figure any other way to stop the old preacher, they locked him away in exile on the prison island of Patmos. Alone in the rocky caves, we find him in fellowship with God.

"I, John, am your brother and your partner in suffering in God's Kingdom and in the patient endurance to which Jesus calls us. I was exiled to the island of Patmos for preaching the word of God and for my testimony about Jesus. It was the Lord's Day, and I was worshiping in the Spirit."

Revelation 1:9-10 NLT

We cannot overlook that simple statement. Alone, John was not alone! There was no clergy around him. There were no deacons to provide support. Cold rocks were the pews and there were no stained-glass windows. Without the benefit of a worship team or a choir, John declared that he was with Jesus. This is incredibly powerful and revealing. It is also a direct example of Christ fulfilling His promise to all of them.

"And be sure of this: I am with you always, even to the end of the age."

Matthew 28:20b NLT

For too many, these words are comforting in the same way that a warm sentiment in a greeting card is comforting. It is a nice thought. It is often a reminder with the same weight as a well-meaning friend saying, "You are not alone." For the believer, it is so much more than this. Jesus was not being sentimental or philosophical. He was not encouraging positive thinking or reaffirming self-talk. He was declaring the awesome fact that the Spirit of God dwells in the life of every true Christian and because of that fact, we are never alone. As we discussed earlier, the presence of His Spirit makes each of us a temple of God. We are the meeting place because He lives within us. That fellowship is available at any moment and during every storm or trial. Learning to abide in our fellowship with Christ is the pathway to joy in all circumstances and seasons.

One Old Testament prophet who ministered during a truly difficult time was Habakkuk. The people of God were besieged by enemies and their hearts were rebellious.

Everything looked fairly bleak and the prophet's eyes did not find anything that produced hope or happiness. Listen to his words in that time of challenge.

> *"Even though the fig trees have no blossoms, and there are no grapes on the vines; even though the olive crop fails, and the fields lie empty and barren; even though the flocks die in the fields, and the cattle barns are empty, yet I will rejoice in the Lord! I will be joyful in the God of my salvation! The Sovereign Lord is my strength! He makes me as surefooted as a deer, able to tread upon the heights."*
>
> *Habakkuk 3:17-19 NLT*

How can a person find joy in God amidst constant hardship and difficulty? When trouble and lack surround us everywhere we look, where do we find the strength to rejoice? Is this old prophet simply deceiving himself, trying to appear spiritual? He tells us where he finds the source of his joy in this passage, but we often miss it. "The Sovereign Lord is my strength!" The Hebrew word for *my strength* is in the first-person singular sense. He is saying, "God is here with me right now and makes me strong." This is not an idea about God. This is a man walking with God. His strength and joy are found in communion with the Lord of his salvation. From that place of fellowship, he finds joy despite the circumstances surrounding him.

> *"He who dwells in the secret place of the Most High shall abide under the shadow of the Almighty. I will say of the Lord, 'He is my refuge and my fortress; my God, in Him I will trust.'"*
>
> *Psalms 91:1-2 NKJV*

This is the promise that was proven true by every faithful person you read about in your Bible. From Abraham to Malachi, the truth of this promise is revealed. David wrote about it in his psalms. Elijah lived it as he walked closely with God. Enoch experienced it so profoundly that he was taken directly to Heaven. Daniel discovered it in the secret place during his time in Babylon. Young Samuel learned of it in the temple. Joshua drew wisdom and strength to lead from the secret place, a lesson he learned from Moses, who stayed there until his face radiated with God's glory. Noah, surrounded by rebellion and sin, kept his heart aligned with God through communion in the secret place, where he received instructions to build the ark. In that same secret place, Moses was shown how to construct the ark of the covenant. Solomon, too, found his inspiration for building the temple in the secret place. It is there, in communion with God, that the faithful find direction, strength, and purpose. Only in fellowship with the Lord can we overcome. This vital truth is obscured by religion even while it is announced in nearly every page of scripture. Isaiah declared it more clearly than most.

"I am overwhelmed with joy in the Lord my God! For he has dressed me with the clothing of salvation and draped me in a robe of righteousness."

Isaiah 61:10 NLT

Another prophet declared joy even though the hour in which he served was dark and difficult. We see this throughout the Old Testament. Those who truly walked with God were in fellowship with Him. From that *secret place,* they all accessed the power of Heaven and prevailed. We celebrate their victories and speak of their lives to this day. The testimony of the Lord points us to the lives of people that knew Him and searched for His face. That relationship was His desire for us.

Jesus shocked the religious leaders of His time by declaring this relationship. It infuriated them for Him to suggest that God wanted to know everyone. Their identity was rooted in the belief that God only wanted fellowship with them because they were holy and better than others. The words of Jesus, when spoken in the context of the example He set with His life, made them angry enough to kill Him.

> *"Jesus replied, 'All who love me will do what I say. My Father will love them, and we will come and make our home with each of them.'"*
>
> *John 14:23 NLT*

Notice the two relational concepts taught here. He looks for those who *love* Him. Rather than elevating perfect ritual practice and theological knowledge, He calls attention to a heart that loves. True love becomes the motivation for any obedience. This was in direct contrast to the self-promotion at the root of religious acts of obedience. It was also promised to be the catalyst to an abiding relationship with God and Christ that was the building of a *home* together. Also, notice who is moving in the statement. "We will come and make our home" announces the Father moving toward the person who loves Jesus. This relationship is His idea. The promise of knowing God was at the center of the Kingdom message that

Jesus was preaching. While the religious desired the praises of men because of their impeccable knowledge about God, Jesus was promising average men and women the doorway to knowing God themselves.

> *"Those who obey God's commandments remain in fellowship with him, and he with them. And we know he lives in us because the Spirit he gave us lives in us."*
>
> 1 John 3:24 NLT

Someone reads that and says, "See, it does say that God only fellowships with the obedient one!" It does say that, but it also tells us the commandments that God is focused on. We will back up and include the verse before this one.

> *"And this is his commandment: We must believe in the name of his Son, Jesus Christ, and love one another, just as he commanded us. Those who obey God's commandments remain in fellowship with him, and he with them. And we know he lives in us because the Spirit he gave us lives in us."*
>
> 1 John 3:23-24 NLT

Fellowship with God is available to those who believe in Jesus and reflect His love to the other believers! Love is again the primary value expressed. If you truly believe Jesus Christ is the only Son of God and the only way to find forgiveness for your sin, and you love others who believe the same, you are invited to the same walk with God in a relationship that all your Bible heroes enjoyed. That place of relationship is the *secret place,* and from there, all good things flow into our lives. We find our strength and our joy in that place of meeting. We see John enjoying this reality in his lonely cave on Patmos. What followed for him was the Heavens opening and the revelation of Jesus Christ being given to the church. We will always find an open Heaven in the secret place as well. We will not receive another book to add to the Bible, but His reality will enlighten our perspective and we will see our world and our lives through His eyes.

Our *secret place* is the place of our private prayer and devotion with Jesus.

Any believer who fails to prioritize these meetings will fall woefully short of the fullness of life that Jesus promised. In our modern times, no ancient Christian practice has been more deemphasized and marginalized than private prayer. Every follower of Yahweh in the Old Testament, along with every follower of Jesus in the New Testament, modeled this truth for the world to see. We simply cannot walk with a God Who we do not know, and we will not know God better without spending time with Him. It is true in all of our other relationships, and our relationship with our Creator and Savior is no different.

"When you pray, don't be like the hypocrites who love to pray publicly on street corners and in the synagogues where everyone can see them. I tell you the truth, that is all the reward they will ever get. But when you pray, go away by yourself, shut the door behind you, and pray to your Father in private. Then your Father, who sees everything, will reward you."

AMAZED AGAIN

Matthew 6:5-6 NLT

Jesus' invitation is truly remarkable when you stop to think about it. The God who is Lord of Heaven and Earth, the Creator who spoke light into existence and raised His Son from the dead, wants to meet with you and me—personally and privately. Imagine having a one-on-one audience with the King of all creation. It's a privilege that is both humbling and awe-inspiring.

Think of all the important people in our world who would not give either of us a minute of their time. The God Who sends demons trembling from His holiness has washed us so clean from sin that He extends an invitation to meet with Him any time. Our fellowship is with God and with His Son, Jesus. Jesus is the One Who instructed us to go away alone, close our door, and meet with God in private. Why is it called the *secret place*? There are many possible reasons, but one primary one is that it is a *secret*. When our meetings with God take place according to His Word, no other person is aware that it is happening. Our relationship with God is reflected outward from our hearts and lives. We begin to shine with His light. People see that, but they do not hear it. Light is silent. When they see enough, they will come and ask about where it comes from. Our focus should be on the relationship with Him.

King David ran into his secret place often. In Psalms 16 he wrote a song about it.

"Keep me safe, O God, for I have come to you for refuge. I said to the Lord, 'You are my Master! Every good thing I have comes from you.' The godly people in the land are my true heroes!

THE SECRET PLACE

I take pleasure in them! Troubles multiply for those who chase after other gods. I will not take part in their sacrifices of blood or even speak the names of their gods. Lord you alone are my inheritance, my cup of blessing. You guard all that is mine. The land you have given me is a pleasant land. What a wonderful inheritance! I will bless the Lord who guides me; even at night my heart instructs me. I know the Lord is always with me. I will not be shaken, for he is right beside me. No wonder my heart is glad, and I rejoice. My body rests in safety. For you will not leave my soul among the dead or allow your holy one to rot in the grave. You will show me the way of life, granting me the joy of your presence and the pleasures of living with you forever."

Psalms 16:1-11 NLT

In our secret place of prayer, we are touching the world that is to come. The peace enjoyed by those already in Heaven is released into our hearts. The perspective of those dwelling above is restored in our spirits. The strength waiting there, far beyond death and disease, is measured back into our lives. Likewise, the *joy* of those abiding in God's presence is shared with us when we pray. We are accessing the life of the Kingdom of God and that is righteousness, peace, and joy. In meeting with the Lord, we encounter His joy, which is our strength. We would be turning the page on this topic too quickly if we did not remind ourselves of the experience of Jesus in this regard. Alone in the garden, with His friends asleep, Jesus secretly prayed to the Father.

"He walked away, about a stone's throw, and knelt down and prayed, 'Father, if you are willing, please take this cup of suf-

fering away from me. Yet I want your will to be done, not mine.' Then an angel from heaven appeared and strengthened him."

Luke 22:41-43 NLT

Our Lord received the strength and endurance He needed to fulfill the Father's will of dying on the cross in His place of secret prayer. With nobody watching except His Father, He reached out and accessed the Kingdom of Heaven. From this place of sacred fellowship, Christ moved toward His destiny with resolve and unwavering commitment. His perspective was restored, giving Him victory over His natural bodily desire to run from this sacrifice. The power to obey and follow the Lord when our natural man wants to run the other way is something we all need. We all find it in the same place Jesus did, the secret place of prayer. The writer of Hebrews indicates He also saw forward into what was next.

"We do this by keeping our eyes on Jesus, the champion who initiates and perfects our faith. Because of the joy awaiting him, he endured the cross, disregarding its shame. Now he is seated in the place of honor beside God's throne."

Hebrews 12:2 NLT

In the secret place, Jesus received strength. He received grace. He was ministered to by angels from Heaven. He also gazed ahead and was able to behold and be reminded of the immense joy that would be His forever when it was all over. May we all realize that our redemption was not intended to give us a relationship with our church. A relationship with our God was the goal and the purpose. From that place of abiding relationship, we too can access strength to endure, grace to obey, and joy to carry us past our pain and hardship. Reclaim your joy in Jesus by meeting with Him again in your own *secret place*. He is waiting to meet with you!

CHAPTER THIRTEEN REFLECTION QUESTIONS

"Religion versus relationship."

1. What is the dynamic between information and experience in the life of a believer?
2. What lessons can you draw from the example of the Apostle John and his fellowship with Jesus?
3. How would you describe to another person the difference between having knowledge of God and truly walking with God?
4. What does scripture reveal about God's desire for all of us?
5. How do you respond to the statement, "You are invited to the same walk with God in relationship that all your Bible heroes enjoyed"?
6. What spiritual strengths do we have access to from our place of private prayer?

"Joy does not simply happen to us. We have to choose joy and keep choosing it every day."

—Henri Nouwen

CHAPTER FOURTEEN

BECOME AMAZED AGAIN

Joy is a hallmark of our faith—vibrant, unmistakable evidence of our salvation. Reclaiming the joy of our salvation has been our focus because joy should overflow naturally as a source of hope in every believer's life. But let's be honest: joy doesn't sustain itself effortlessly. We must make a deliberate choice to claim the joy that is rightfully ours and stand firm against anything that threatens to diminish it, whether it comes from within or from outside influences. We've explored countless scriptures that equip us to live this out. Why is this so important? Because joy makes our witness more compelling, strengthens us to endure life's trials, and—most importantly—is something Jesus Himself desires for us to experience. Joy isn't just a feeling; it's a transformative gift we're called to embrace.

> *"I have told you these things so that you will be filled with my joy. Yes, your joy will overflow!"*
>
> *John 15:11 NLT*

AMAZED AGAIN

One of my favorite stories from the book of Acts is an occurrence from very early in the growth of the new Church. The apostles were moving in the power of the Holy Spirit and many people were healed. It was clear that the same power that had been with Jesus was now with His followers. This was terribly alarming to the priests and officials. They had hoped all of this new talk would die with Jesus when they convinced the Romans to kill Him. Instead, there were now multiple people moving around town and doing even more miracles! In anger they arrest the apostles and put them in the public jail. God, Who I believe has a sense of humor, sends an angel to set them free during the night. In the morning, these officials summon them from the jail so they can intimidate and persecute them and are informed they are gone! Can you imagine their embarrassment and frustration? While they are still finding out what happened at the jail, another person runs in and informs them the apostles are standing in the temple courts and preaching Jesus. We see men who knew they were set free with a purpose. That is something that all within the Church should keep in mind as well.

The apostles are again brought before the counsel. They rebuke the apostles and seek to humiliate them. In their anger, they give a wonderful report of the apostles effectiveness when they announce, "You have filled Jerusalem with your teaching about Him [Jesus]." Peter provides all sermon writers throughout history with an amazing statement to work with and informs the counsel, "We must obey God rather than human authority." This is simply too much for these Jewish leaders to endure, and so, in fury, they decide to kill them all. Thankfully one older Pharisee is able to bring some calm and wisdom to the group. The other elders decided to listen to him. Instead of killing them, they flogged them and commanded them never to preach about Jesus again. It is the description of their departure that makes me smile every time I read it.

> *"The apostles left the high council rejoicing that God had counted them worthy to suffer disgrace for the name of Jesus."*
>
> Acts 5:41 NLT

Rejoicing is the verb associated with joy. When we have enough joy to motivate our actions with joyful expressions, we are rejoicing. These men were flogged. That was no small thing. Strong and violent soldiers tore their backs apart with leather whips. They walked away bleeding profusely and needing medical care. One of the main points of this punishment was to make it obvious to everyone that you had been disciplined. Their robes were most likely shredded. Half naked and bleeding, these men walked, or possibly limped, down the streets of Jerusalem. It was intended to send the message that following this man, Jesus, only led to personal pain and hardship. The natural human response would be anger and humiliation. Yet, joy was so intense within them that we find them rejoicing! Picture them laughing and encouraging one another as they lift their hands and give God glory. I often wonder if James was thinking of them when he wrote the following.

> *"Dear brothers and sisters, when troubles of any kind come your way, consider it an opportunity for great joy."*
>
> James 1:2 NLT

Most of us do not run face-first into a big pile of trouble and immediately see it as an opportunity to rejoice. James goes on to teach that the joy flows from having an eternal perspective about this life rather than focusing on temporary circumstances. The trouble will pass away. The strength and growth it produces in me enables me to make this journey to the end. For that reason, I should rejoice in trouble. Every one of these punished apostles followed Jesus with even more boldness. In short order, they left Jerusalem and took their lessons of joy and endurance into every corner of the Roman world.

The abuse intended to silence them only made their voices louder. Their flesh was torn but their spirits were strengthened.

I believe this will become increasingly important for all of us in the coming months and years. The hatred of Christ and His actual followers is increasing. The Lord warned us of this condition in the last days. He already told us that the momentary season of popularity the church has enjoyed will end. Hatred for the truth, and any that proclaim it, will grow to the point of violence. No matter how deeply we long for peace with the world, the moment we refuse to turn away from Him, the world will inevitably turn against us.

"Even those closest to you—your parents, brothers, relatives, and friends—will betray you. They will even kill some of you. And everyone will hate you because you are my followers."

Luke 21:16-17 NLT

This hatred and betrayal will mean trouble for all of us alive at this time. We have all experienced people who dislike us because of our faith or what they think it implies about our politics. We have all had our witness rejected and seen a person get offended by what we are sharing. These events are opportunities to grow in joy and endurance because what is ahead for us will be far more difficult.

"Then you will be arrested, persecuted, and killed. You will be hated all over the world because you are my followers. And many will turn away from me and betray and hate each other. And many false prophets will appear and will deceive many people. Sin will be rampant everywhere, and the love of many will grow cold. But the one who endures to the end will be saved."

Matthew 24:9-13 NLT

Without diving deep into eschatology, let me say that for decades, Bible teachers have used various techniques of interpretation to tell us that we will escape all these problems. Today, all of these things are happening to Christians all over the world. Even if you are reading this from the comfort of a peaceful nation that appears to welcome all beliefs, you can surely see the tide shifting. Just last week, I read the account of a man arrested for "hate speech" in a European country. His "hate speech" was declaring what the Bible says about a particular cultural issue. When he refused to stop, he was jailed. Once in jail, his family reported he was persecuted by other prisoners who learned of his Christian worldview. If left in that situation, it will be a short journey to one of them killing him. This is precisely what Jesus warned us about.

Let me remind you that people who hate the truth will also hate those who proclaim it. That hatred will bring trouble to our front door. If that happens, will we be able to walk away rejoicing?

"Rejoice in our confident hope. Be patient in trouble, and keep on praying."

Romans 12:12 NLT

Keep on praying again reminds us that in the secret place of our personal communion with Christ, we find what we need. To be patient in trouble implies understanding that it will pass. Our joy is found in focusing more on our hope in Jesus than we do on the trouble we are walking through. I am not making light of persecution and martyrdom, but for a believer, even death is a temporary problem. Our hope is anchored in Jesus and the eternal life He has provided.

Few endured as much trouble and hatred as the Apostle Paul. As a former Pharisee, he was seen as the ultimate traitor to their order, and their hatred for him overflowed numerous times. His faith never provided him an exemption from these hardships. As he walked through the various fires of persecution, he developed a perspective on what he endured that we must examine before we are finished. Listen to his testimony.

"We know that God, who raised the Lord Jesus, will also raise us with Jesus and present us to himself together with you. All of this is for your benefit. And as God's grace reaches more and more people, there will be great thanksgiving, and God will receive more and more glory. That is why we never give up. Though our bodies are dying, our spirits are being renewed every

day. *For our present troubles are small and won't last very long. Yet they produce for us a glory that vastly outweighs them and will last forever! So we don't look at the troubles we can see now; rather, we fix our gaze on things that cannot be seen. For the things we see now will soon be gone, but the things we cannot see will last forever."*

2 Corinthians 4:14-18 NLT

Gazing at *unseen eternal things* is what all of this has been about. Joy is ours to possess, but it is found in eternal truth. It is found in the reality of Jesus living within us. The Word of God revealed to us brings joy home again in waves. Reminding ourselves of His unshakeable Kingdom and the beautiful family of faith we belong to restores our joy as well. Every victory over our adversary's desire to destroy us adds fuel to that fire. When we look again at the cross and see our Savior loving us enough to die so we could be adopted, our value to Him causes rejoicing. When we truly worship Jesus and humbly serve others who worship Him, our joy multiplies. When our memories fade, even slightly, we are invited to the table for communion that we might remember Him again. If we have understood His desire for relationship with us, we are daily coming into the secret place and enjoying fellowship with our Redeemer. All of these realities enable us to reclaim and retain our joy as we walk through trouble.

Living amazed by Jesus is the key. Finding our way back to the place of being amazed by Jesus is the answer. To love Him with all of our heart, mind, soul, and strength was the most important commandment ever given to us by God. Does He amaze you right now? Before you give a religiously precise and expected answer, you owe it to yourself and Jesus to reflect honestly. We all have to do this. Sitting here and writing this, I must ask myself if I am amazed by Jesus. If I see Him for Who He is and all that He has done, I will be amazed. If I am not, I have lost sight of Him somewhere in the busyness and challenges of this life. Every time I realize this has happened, I must turn my eyes toward Him again if I want to walk in the joy of my salvation. All my joy is found in Him. All of your joy is found in Him as well. Please do not allow this world to take it from you. Do not allow cold religion or ritual to replace it. Do not allow duty and responsibility to mask its decline. Allow joy to help you measure the health of your heart and the fidelity of your relationship with Christ.

> *"How amazing are the deeds of the Lord! All who delight in him should ponder them. Everything he does reveals his glory and majesty. His righteousness never fails. He causes us to remember his wonderful works. How gracious and merciful is our Lord!"*
>
> *Psalms 111:2-4 NLT*

> *"You love him even though you have never seen him. Though you do not see him now, you trust him; and you rejoice with a glorious, inexpressible joy. The reward for trusting him will be the salvation of your souls."*
>
> *1 Peter 1:8-9 NLT*

Allow me to encourage you from personal experience that all of this works. These are not Bible study theories presented to you as concepts. I have only included admonitions that I have benefited from in my own walk. We all have challenges to our joy as we follow the Lord. My family has had our share. Jesus has faithfully met me in these ways and restored my joy more times than I have room here to recount. From experience, I can assure you that if you have been betrayed and wounded by your fellow Christians, these ideas will allow you to recover with joy. If you are in a season where nothing seems to be going your way, these ideas will help you continue on with joy. If you have wept as one of your children abandoned faith and family, these ideas will help you find joy while watching the road for their return. If persistent health problems refuse to retreat, no matter how much you pray, you can still reclaim your joy in Christ. All of this I know for certain.

Along the way worship has been deepened in my heart. These wonderful aspects of God's faithfulness have become a part of our worship culture. David would encounter the goodness of God and sing about it. A few years back, I decided to do the same. The goal of writing music should never be to compete or obtain notoriety.

> **Worship *in spirit and in truth* encompasses the unity of what the Word of God teaches and how we have seen that manifest in our lives.**

The Christian Church has been blessed with hundreds of wonderful anthems of praise throughout the centuries. One could ask if there is any need to keep writing new songs. My answer is an unflinching "Yes!" Every writer has a journey that inspires songs of worship and trust. Every congregation makes a sojourn through the land and seeks to follow the Lord. That journey inspires worship as well. Our personal songs will almost certainly never be the famous Christian hits that hundreds of other congregations will sing, but that is not the point. Each one born from sincere gratitude for God's faithfulness deepens our experience in our own secret place as we fellowship with Christ. If you take any time to listen to what I have written, my only hope is that it inspires you to write your own song. Then God will be glorified more and more.

> *"Always be full of joy in the Lord. I say it again—rejoice!"*
>
> *Philippians 4:4 NLT*

Remember my happy singing friend? He went home to be with Jesus far too young for any of us who knew him. He kept his joy for the entire journey. His family suffered losses like all families do. He experienced significant setbacks in his career and saw his income plummet. Relocation was required and in the new city there were even more struggles. No longer in his familiar little church, he found his way to the choir at a larger church where he continued his happy singing. One day he sat down at home following a basketball game in his driveway and died. It was so sudden that we were all left in shock. He was healthy and had no known issues to give anyone any warning. All of us who knew him gathered at the larger church for his funeral. In a large crowd, I found myself listening as others shared about knowing him. Soon, I was smiling through my own tears. One after another, people reported "he was always happy." Following the service, one member of their congregation told me that no matter what she was going through, she would look up at the choir and see the huge smile on his face as they praised the Lord. He held his joy in his heart to the very end. It was a fun, full-circle moment for me. His joy inspired me when we met and inspired me again when he left.

> **Our world is growing darker and colder.
> To shine for our Savior, we need our joy.**

The joy we have in Christ shines like a lighthouse on a rocky coastline as the storms of this eroding culture batter the lost around us. When speaking prophetically about the future redemption coming to mankind by God's Messiah, Isaiah told us this.

"You will live in joy and peace. The mountains and the hills will burst into song, and the trees of the field will clap their hands! Where once there were thorns, cypress trees will grow. Where nettles grew, myrtles will sprout up. These events will bring great honor to the Lord's name; they will be an everlasting sign of his power and love."

Isaiah 55:12-13 NLT

Our joy is a sign of His power and love. Our peace is as well. The praise and the songs that erupt from the earth are a sign. The growth of new and pleasing fruit where the thorns and nettles grew is a sign. All this brings great honor to the Lord's Name! God is glorified in our lives by our faithfulness and our obedience. He is glorified when we choose holiness over sin. He is glorified when we serve others instead of ourselves. He is also glorified when we walk through this broken world full of His joy as we hope in His Kingdom and look for His return. Let all of us who know Jesus reclaim our joy! Let it shine each and every day. Every time a person asks where it originates from, we will faithfully point them to the loving Savior Who has been so incredibly faithful to all of us. May the Lord bless you as you live for Him.

CHAPTER FOURTEEN REFLECTION QUESTIONS

"Why is my joy hiding?"

1. When was the last time you sincerely rejoiced and what inspired it?
2. How does having an eternal perspective about circumstances influence our ability to have joy during difficult times?
3. What will be the root cause of the increasing animosity toward the followers of Jesus as we navigate the last days?
4. Why did the Jewish leaders so hate the Apostle Paul? Are there relationships in your life that are similar to how he was treated?
5. How do you respond to the statement, "Joy is ours to possess, but it is found in eternal truth"?
6. How can the presence of joy help us analyze the fidelity of our relationship with Christ?
7. How can abundant and visible joy impact our Christian witness as we walk through this world?

"The Lord looked into the depth of my being with great kindness; I thought I would die for joy under that gaze."

—Saint Faustina

CONCLUSION

When I reflect on it now, everything seems very straightforward. Joy is found in a deep relationship with Jesus. The church is not a substitute for that. When we establish our essential connection to the church, we do not experience the full measure of joy. We may find enjoyable relationships with others. We may discover a worship culture we appreciate. We may find a speaker or teacher we admire. As wonderful as all of that may be, it is not the same as being continually filled with His joy.

Why wouldn't the fullness of joy flow from God's heart through the church and into our hearts? The answer is simple.

Jesus didn't make the ultimate sacrifice for sin just so that mankind could form organizations called churches. His goal was our restored relationship with Him.

We find that the fullness of joy is in that relationship because it brings joy to His heart. We end up rejoicing in the overflow of the joy He has for us!

Having a relationship with a church is easier. We know exactly when and where to go. We typically know what will happen before it does, so there are no surprises. Most importantly, we are in control because we decide whether or not to go to church. Whenever we have a different priority, there's no one to question it. Everything is quite neat and tidy. The level of impact that relationship has on us is mainly determined by us. It also does not stem from the overflowing joy in Christ's heart.

Attending church truly has a Heaven-sent essence when it stems from a week spent walking with Jesus. In that moment, I go to worship because of the incredible ways He has revealed Himself throughout the week. I have a desire to learn His ways, as I've uncovered a limitation within myself while walking with Him during that time. My focus also extends to others because He has been speaking to me about them as I prayed for them throughout the week. The weekly church meeting transforms into an extension of the work of the Kingdom of God. Jesus is my connection, and at that point, church becomes optional. I no longer adhere to the religious notion that simply being there equates to being "with Him" in intimate and vibrant fellowship.

If you lack joy and confidently identify yourself as a born-again Christian, it's time to examine your relationship with the Lord closely.

CONCLUSION

The joy of the Lord should be our strength, and as He strengthens us, we live in the overflow of His joy. If we find it missing, we may soon realize we have substituted religion for relationship. Our relationship may be with our church instead of our Christ. We may be investing all our time in being there rather than being "with Him."

The great lie that almost immediately grips our minds is, "I don't have time!" We have become accustomed to using time as our excuse. I challenge all of us to confront this lie head-on. We will discover that we do not lack time for a relationship with Jesus. We will realize that we allow our time to be wasted and consumed by other priorities. We will find that we are often "making time" for others while claiming we have no time for Him. This is the sinister trap set by our enemy. In the end, we find ourselves joyless and tired. We become weary and disillusioned. We live in the overflow of other people's opinions and judgments rather than in the joy of our Savior.

Turn it around and seek the Lord. Start small if you need to. Cut out one streaming episode and replace it with prayer in a space free of cellphones or tablets. Keep a Bible near your coffee pot and read while it brews. Find something spiritually uplifting to listen to while you're working out. Whenever you're alone, have a conversation with Christ. Connect with Him. Listen to Him. Take His advice and follow His guidance. Call on Him before you call anyone else. He is your Redeemer! Everyone else is just your audience.

If you eliminate every activity related to or centered on your church from your week, how much of your "relationship" with Jesus remains? This thought is a struggle for many because a church they like has become the environment where their faith exists. Everything outside of "church" is merely a world they try to survive until they can return to church. At church, every aspect of Christianity is easy. The band helps us worship, and the preacher guides our thinking. We even get told when to pray. At home, all of this is simply a decision we make based on our love and devotion to Jesus. What that reveals about our heart for Him is the truth about ourselves that we must examine. When did we last sit and talk with Jesus?

My sincere prayer for you as we conclude this journey is that you have found some inspiration to reconnect with Him.

He is truly amazing. If you have lost your joy in knowing Him, I pray you find your way back to the overflow of His joy for you. I pray you are amazed by Him again—get amazed and stay amazed. Do whatever it takes to remain close to Jesus. Make your relationship with Him the most important one in your life. May blessings and joy be yours in abundance. Amen.

CONCLUSION

CONCLUSION REFLECTION QUESTIONS

"I am here for my joy, please."

1. When was the last time you felt a deep sense of joy in your relationship with Christ? What moments or experiences brought it to life?
2. Can you identify specific situations or patterns where your joy began to fade? What might have contributed to this?
3. In what ways has your connection with Jesus influenced your daily life and restored your joy?
4. Which scriptures have encouraged or renewed your joy in the past? How might revisiting them deepen your connection with Him?
5. Are there habits or distractions in your life that hinder your joy? What practical steps can you take to address them?
6. How can you intentionally share the joy of Christ with someone in your life this week?
7. What daily practices or reminders could help you maintain a lasting sense of joy rooted in Christ?

ABOUT THE AUTHOR

Walter Hill is a dedicated pastor in Wyoming with over 25 years of experience navigating the highs and lows of faith and ministry. He is passionate about helping others rediscover the enduring joy that comes from a deep relationship with Jesus Christ. Walter's journey, shaped by personal trials such as loss, long-term illness in loved ones, and challenges in ministry, serves as the foundation for his heartfelt guidance and teachings.

Walter married his high school sweetheart, and together they have embarked on an incredible journey, recently celebrating their 34th anniversary. They have two adult children and have now entered the world of grandparenthood with the birth of their first grandchild. Walt's wife says she married him because he could make her laugh, while he believes he won her over with his dashing good looks. They continue to discuss this apparent inconsistency in their accounts.

Music is one of Walt's other loves. He plays several instruments and writes and performs his own songs. He still entertains the idea of starting an 80s hair metal cover band made up entirely of older men without hair. When he is not fulfilling his various church responsibilities, he also serves his community as a hospice chaplain.

Through his relatable storytelling and profound insights, Walter inspires readers to reclaim their hope, strengthen their faith, and embrace the abundant life Christ offers. His book, *Amazed Again*, is a testament to his passion for guiding others on the path to lasting joy in a world that often fades.

CONNECT WITH WALT

WalterHill40@proton.me
WalterHill.net

www.ingramcontent.com/pod-product-compliance
Lightning Source LLC
Chambersburg PA
CBHW070135080526
44586CB00015B/1705